french girl knits

ACCESSORIES

french girl knits

ACCESSORIES

modern designs for a beautiful life

kristeen griffin-grimes

INTERWEAVE
interweave.com

Interweave Press LLC
201 East Fourth Street
Loveland, CO 80537-5655 USA
interweave.com

Printed in China by Asia Pacific Offset Ltd.

Library of Congress Cataloging-in-Publication Data

Griffin-Grimes, Kristeen, 1947-
French girl accessories : modern designs for a beautiful life /
 Kristeen Griffin-Grimes.
pages cm
Includes bibliographical references and index.
ISBN 978-1-59668-490-4 (pbk.)
1. Knitting--Patterns. 2. Dress accessories--Patterns. I. Title.
TT825.G68353 2012
746.432--dc23
2012002878

10 9 8 7 6 5 4 3 2 1

EDITOR Ann Budd

TECHNICAL EDITOR Lori Gayle

ART DIRECTOR Liz Quan

PHOTOGRAPHER Rain Griffin Blond

PHOTO STYLISTS Amanda Carter Gomes, Kristeen Griffin-Grimes

COVER & INTERIOR DESIGN Karla Baker

ILLUSTRATION Gayle Ford

HAIR & MAKEUP Lindsey Watkins

PRODUCTION Katherine Jackson

merci beaucoup!

"Thank you" always seems like a meager phrase when expressing my gratitude for the stellar assemblage of artists that helped me compile this book. As always, Team Interweave has provided me with a rock-solid foundation on which to stand and let me take wing with my flights of fancy—my debt to all of them is completely immeasurable! Extra special *mille merci* goes out to Allison Korleski and Marlene Blessing for rekindling my desire to put together this second book and for our wild brainstorming sessions, complete with literal and figurative woolgathering! Former Editorial Director Tricia Waddell will always hold a place in my heart for being the shepherd of my first book, *French Girl Knits*. Thank you to Steve Koenig and Marilyn Murphy for always believing in my off-the-cuff designing . . . *merci!* Huge hugs and thanks to Art Director Liz Quan, who was down in the trenches with us through all the photo-shoot madness (and still had energy to party with us afterward); you are always welcome to crash our family dinners under the fig tree! To the Interweave crew whom I've yet to meet, the graphic designers, marketers, and those who labor daily without fanfare, my (knitted) *chapeau* is off to you—what wonderful work you do!

I would have been seriously lost in this project without my editor, Ann Budd, whose calm hand has always guided me and smoothed off every rough edge—I can never repay you for your patience (perhaps a home-cooked meal *à la française* here in Seattle). And what would I have done without my tech editor-to-end-all-tech-editors, Lori Gayle, who

took the scribble and scraps of patterns that I offered and produced a cogent, clear, and dare I say, sublimely refined version that would be a joy for anyone to knit . . . thank you a thousand times over, Ann and Lori!

And speaking of family, for four riotous, joyful, super-charged days, my French Girl family put together a photo shoot at our little urban oasis in Seattle that was homegrown elegance at its best. We fluffed and curated, pinned and primped, wrangled and went more than the extra mile to make something enduring and beautiful.

I don't think I have ever seen my immensely talented daughter, Rain Griffin Blond, work so hard. She continued to amaze me with her strength of character and loving focus, not only through the eye of her camera as she took one ex-quisite photo after another, but in her passionate dedication to helping me achieve my vision. That she poured herself into the project with every ounce of energy she had and pro-duced the dreamy images you see in this book, is a special talent, and I love her fiercely for it—*Je t'aime, chérie!*

Our cohorts in this endeavor were many: the brilliant Amanda Carter Gomes who produced our photo shoot with such style and grace that it would not have been the same without her. Amanda has a quick mind and a generous heart, a combination that one does not find very often; her mark is on every photo you will see in this book and I am honored to call her a friend and sister artist. Lindsey Watkins, our hair and makeup guru, is a genius . . . that is all I have to say . . . and one of the most imaginative and playful creatures I have ever known (one Leo lady to another).

When we were musing about the models for the designs within these pages, we hit the jackpot! Sophie Barnett-Dyer with her depth of emotive expression and gentle elegance,

Kim Crayton, whose calm energy and powerful presence was so welcome, and finally, the lovely Jordan Lily Alban-Vallat, whom our family has known since childhood, for bringing us a wise-beyond-her-years stillness and a true golden glow. You all made ev-erything look even better than I could have imagined! Ladies, you rock!

My own dear family pulled out all the stops. Darling Adri-enne who made sure we were well fed, our son Deva and *beau-fils* Jeremiah, who provided loads of behind-the-scenes moral sup-port, and, finally, my one-and-only husband, Phil, a man who has always been there for me in so many ways, who unques-tionably did whatever was asked and with a good spirit. How fortunate I am to be a part of this creative, impassioned group of people! Special love goes to Soni Davé-Schock and Henri Schock, owners of Bottlehouse in our Madrona neighborhood for the use of their charming wine bar during the photo shoot and to my sample knitters, Michelle Strakeljahn Mauer and Taryn Nikolic . . . *merci, mes amis!*

And finally, thanks to you, my faithful readers and knit-ters, for making up my designs and supporting me through my books, Etsy shoppes, and tours in La Belle France.

je vous remercie!
kristeen

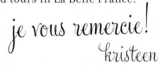

contents

la vie Quotidienne

A LOOK AT FRENCH DAILY LIFE AND STYLE

Ask any French woman what she considers the most invaluable items in her closet and unfailingly the response is *Les Accessoires*—The Accessories! In concert with a classic little black dress, vintage Chanel handbag, and perfectly tailored coat, you'll find a treasure trove of scarves, wraps, bags, gloves, and, thankfully now, especially among the younger *femmes françaises*, a collection of knitted hats that run the gamut from *trés chic* berets to funky, slouchy Rasta-styled caps. My French friends' scarves, shrugs, gloves, and socks alone would need a Dewey decimal system to catalog them, with names that reflect a more elegant time—*écharpe, gilet, châle, cache-coeur, foulard, mitaines, gants, chaussettes, toque, pantoufles, cloche, bonnets, snood*—just reading them makes one want to slip on a *cache-coeur* and sneak out for a martini at an elegant hotel.

We knitters are fortunate that handmade is cool again (although we always knitted through the cool and not-so-cool times as well) and that we have mastered a craft that gives us the freedom to create stunning one-of-a-kind garments. With just a few balls of delicious yarn and some perseverance, our handiwork can whip up a multitude of accessories that add the consummate finishing touch to our wardrobes. These days, we are party to an international community of brilliant and *au courant* knitters through websites such as Ravelry (ravelry.com), a bevy of edifying knitting blogs (some of my favorites are listed in the Bibliography), and Facebook. There is never a lack of inspiration or support. Indeed, these are fine times to be a knitter!

Because this is a book about accessories, and the French do accessories so very well, perhaps you will indulge me the following small personal treatise on French Style (with a capital S) and how it relates to what we choose to wear (and knit). I offer this as what one American woman has learned from traveling and living among the French. It is profoundly easy to glamorize another culture—and I've done that aplenty with my French musings—but I've also come to realize that there are reasons why the French have developed such a well-defined "look." We can learn from them to make our lives (and the garments we knit) a more authentic reflection of our personal style.

In the grand timeline of world history, America is still a young country—brash and unruly as a teenager and trend-driven to the max. Excitingly innovative and scintillating as that can be, our culture suffers (literally) from a diet of excess: food, goods, information—you name it, and you can find it all with one tiny mouse click. The French have generations upon generations of tastemakers from the Sun

le matin { THE MORNING }

French coffee, heartbreakingly fresh croissants, *confiture fait maison*—ah, the glories of *le petit-déjeuner*. Hardly a pastry passes my lips when I am home in the United States, but for some odd reason, while in France, our family eats whatever we want (like hogs, I am afraid) and still manage to gain not an ounce (in fact, our waistlines shrink). Perhaps it's all that traipsing up the intriguing back streets of ultra-hilly villages or our daily, salty ablutions in the Mediterranean—whatever the magic, I adore the formula and long for it when we return stateside.

I have another (far less satisfying than a croissant) morning ritual—the hunt for the perfect hat, scarf, shrug, etc., to complement what I plan to wear each day. A word of note: my wardrobe is positively Amish—black, gray, pale gray, charcoal (you get the picture)—and I live in a completely white house, so I begin with a neutral palette that begs for a bit of chromatic experimentation.

But, alas, my allergy to color has overtaken every facet of my existence and recently spun out of control when I chose tiny black-and-white chicks to ultimately become our handsome egg-layers. By some fortune, the breed

King to Coco and are well practiced in the art of aesthetics. What is considered good taste (*de bon goût*) has been expertly honed over the centuries. This can be described as elegant, curated, refined, effortless, and, most importantly, timeless.

My husband and I were well schooled on these tenets of French society on a wild cab ride to Charles de Gaulle Airport, careening through the streets of a sleepy, Sunday Paris, where we (very happily) received a 45-minute tutorial on Life *à la Française* in mile-a-minute French from our intrepid driver. We'd asked him, quite innocently, why there was so much that was aesthetically pleasing in France. He obliged, and then some. It was really quite simple. He said, "It is because we care. We care about our past, so we pass down as much of our way of life as we can—from tattered family recipes to how one behaves in public, from the correct way to hold a knife and fork to how to grow a perfect carrot in a small backyard allotment." He explained about the sanctity of the ritual Sunday lunch, where families spend hours talking at the table (that literal French cultural center of the universe). I found myself recalling my own hectic dinners *en famille*, with eight of us squabbling over the last drumstick, and suddenly pined for a bit of Gallic decorum in my childhood.

Let's take a look at a typical French day and how it has affected what I knit and what I choose to knit with.

of hardy French Canadian stock (*Dominque*) I chose were perfectly composed *noir et blanc* feathered ladies that fit splendidly into my color scheme. I am, however, endeavoring to add more colors to my world and have decided that accessories are the sublime solution to this part of my daily routine. If, like me, you are color shy, yet secretly long for a wee more zip in your wardrobe, consider starting with a few accessories knitted in knockout colors from the designs in the upcoming pages. I may join you!

l'après-midi { THE AFTERNOON }

The southern Europeans have the right idea when it comes to the afternoon. They eat, then they rest. *La sieste* (as it is called in France) is a foreign concept to most of us, especially in the early afternoon. My family and I learned this the hard way, when, giving in to jet lag for a few days, we became completely out of sync with the French clock. The cupboards were bare, the noon bell had rung, and every door to every shop, post office, bank, and gas station had snapped shut, so the proprietors could partake in the all-important ritual of *le déjuner* and *la sieste*. Had we been in a larger town, a *brasserie* would have been the solution, since most of the restaurants near us were reserved well ahead of time. We were condemned to wander the picturesque back alleys until a *bistro* owner took pity on us and sandwiched us in between two other tables.

We were just becoming acquainted with France at that time, our language skills were rudimentary at best, and the idea of navigating a wine list, let alone unearthing that sweet marriage of flavors that occurs when the right wine meets its food mate, was far beyond our paltry skills. We were saved and ultimately well educated by a server who obviously adored his country and its wines . . . and those Gallic words of wisdom continue to ring true in many arenas of my life. His advice: Simplify things down to their components, know your raw materials, and most of all, relax. If you make a mistake, the world will not end! We found this practical and down-to-earth counsel most appealing and widely applicable to many situations in life—including knitting.

la nuit { THE NIGHT }

For many of us, nighttime is knitting time. The halcyon hours, when we finally set aside the labors of the day and create something just for ourselves, are few. We cherish these moments.

I am often asked why I knit when knitted garments are hanging on every shop rack from here to Paris? The craft that first began as a path to being thrifty and DIY (do-it-yourself) has lead to something much deeper—artistic satisfaction, to be sure, but also knowing that I am using my time well in the creation of something that will be valued by myself and those to whom I gift my work. I am not a prolific knitter (book-writing duties aside), but I covet artisan-made raw materials in my life and work, from the farmstead cheese on our table to handspun yarns, many of which I can now find in my own environs. The veneration of artisanship in all things became deeply encoded in me during my premier voyage to France and took root, quite simply, during our family's first truly French dining experience.

I had read about that fabled hours-long affair, but nothing prepared me for what was to come. The meal, with its leisurely pace, the conviviality of the guests (all French-speaking vacationers), and our shared appreciation of the exquisitely fresh, lovingly put-together repast, left me with a desire not to settle for the ordinary, be it what I chose for dinner or the next yarn I cast on with. Since that evening, I have had many such meals—in rustic *auberges* tucked deep within the forests of Brittany, by candlelight in the shadow of ruined Loire Valley *chateaux*—and I never cease to remark to my family, "This is so very good!" When we asked our hosts why the food tasted divine, they would smile, shrug their shoulders, and say, "Oh, that cheese came from the small farm one valley over," or "those are from my brother who raises sheep in the salt marshes near the sea."

In the United States, we are re-learning what the Europeans have long celebrated: that our own backyards (literally and figuratively) are where the best stuff of life resides. I am delighted to see a renaissance of interest in regionally produced artisan fare, from garage wines to independent hand-dyed yarns. I would encourage you to seek out those creators of unique and high-caliber goods, purchase that one luxurious skein, and put it to use in a project from this book. Many of the designs use little more than that. Be enthralled by your knitting and revel in the beauty of that single skein.

My desire here is a call to mine our own history, to celebrate daily life (always a good idea), and to develop an appreciation, as the French do, for quality over quantity. It is a gentle self-assuredness that the world is in beautiful and proper order, with neither too little nor too much. It's the knowledge of being supported by a foundation as good and true as the two-millennia-old Roman Road (you can actually feel the weight of this history when you are there). Admittedly, in this sped-up age of social media and global interconnectedness, *le fast food* and *McDo* (a pet name for a certain American food chain), change is swiftly moving through France now, especially among *les jeunes*. And, yet, the aforementioned underpinnings of French culture remain very deep and inspire me daily.

To that end, I encourage you to find what is meaningful to you, to hone your taste, cast aside the fluff, and distill your knitting down to what you really love—which I optimistically hope will include the designs within these pages. Because most of these projects are small and may be completed in a short time, take the opportunity to decompress and enjoy the process of knitting, the steady beat of wood, steel, or bamboo looping an exquisite yarn into something you will truly enjoy.

In my first book, *French Girl Knits* (Interweave, 2009), I spoke about taking pleasure—in a very French way—in the "small moments" in life. I encourage you to do just that with the accessories I've included here. Find a comfortable spot, cosset yourself away from the rush of daily life, and begin, one stitch at a time, to savor the experience.

For *French Girl Knits: Accessories*, I endeavored to create a collection of designs that would tantalize you to pick up your needles and create unique, as well as easy-to-wear, garments—something that would make you feel "well put together," as my mother used to say. Most are quite simple to work up and make perfect weekend projects, such as the Bohème beret (page 42), knitted in satisfyingly bulky yarn or the Gitane *cache-coeur* (page 82), a confection of feathery suri alpaca and merino that is a breeze to knit. Even the more challenging Tattoo inky-hued wrap (page 94) requires just an extra dose of patience and attention for a "Wow-you-knit-that?" payoff.

bon tricot and bon chance in the pursuit of all things wonderful!

Finding Your Perfect Knitted Accessories

To size up your accessories wardrobe and begin knitting garments you will truly treasure (and, ultimately, wear), let us reflect on the words of Madame Chanel: "Fashion fades, style is eternal." I hesitate to dispense fashion advice—I believe in everyone's right to dress exactly as they please with no interference from *la police de la mode*—so my thoughts on the subject are offered in the spirit of assisting you in honing your knitting choices.

To develop your own sense of *la mode* in your knitting, begin with a study of not only what looks good *to* you, but also what looks good *on* you. In the company of a sidekick for wise counsel, take some time to try on various styles of hats, wraps, or shrugs. Use a three-way mirror for viewing—it can be a real eye-opener!

For myself, being of small stature with wide shoulders, raglan-sleeved sweaters, anything with horizontal stripes (as much as I dearly love them), giant cables, or too much fabric or fuss around my neck or front are definite no-goes. Simple fitted styles are best, even in scarves and headwear. I have loads of hair, so I look best in sleek designs that don't overwhelm. Much as I lust after giant cowls and wildly patterned shawls that appeal to my gypsy heart, they end up wearing me, instead of me wearing them!

Take the time to assess your perks and peccadilloes—it will allow you to skip over a sea of designs that you know are not ideal. Uncover and play up your strengths and you'll be on your way to simplifying your knitting life. Don't settle for something that is simply functional—you can have your cake and eat it, too, in a warm hat that is super stylin', *bien sûr*!

Les chapeaux et les toques

HATS AND TOQUES

IT IS BELIEVED THE WORD *CHAPEAU* FIRST ENTERED THE FRENCH LEXICON during the Renaissance and originally sprang from *chaplet*, which signified a wreath worn on the head—a lovely provenance, don't you think? The history of headwear in France is replete with everything from the fancifully ridiculous (the towering ship hat worn by Marie Antoinette comes to mind) to the sleek, simple silhouette of a classic Chanel beret with grosgrain ribbon band.

Sidestepping Marie and her kin, I found a design home in two distinct eras of French fashion for this section—the Revolutionary period and the 1920–1930s. Post-Revolution, as all trappings of the aristocracy were cast aside, both men's and women's headwear returned to a pared-down look with the aesthetic of the common folk in favor. The heavy cotton lace headscarf Jasmin (page 16) captures the spirit of women's everyday wear during that period—an uncomplicated swirl of fabric to tie back the hair for quotidian duties, as practical and stylish then as it is now.

The shape of both Sapphire (page 20) and Coquille (page 26) mimic many of the casual toques worn by both sexes, often sporting a jaunty tricolor ribbon in support of the new regime. The timeless design in Sapphire ultimately

made its way to the New World on the heads of emigrants who departed France during these tumultuous years (my own ancestors included). Coquille will give you the opportunity to try your hand at a combo of brioche stitch and cables in a small, manageable project pulled into its delightfully crumpled shape with artful finishing stitches.

The silhouette of Tulipe (page 32) has always reminded me of the warm felted bed caps worn by gentlemen and peasants alike against the bitter intrusion of night air. With lace worked in the round and a brilliant scarlet hue, this project is a far cry from those pragmatic helmets, but will be just as warming.

In planning for this chapter, I could not overlook berets, the *baguettes* of French hat fashion—iconic and ubiquitous! The humble beret has been worn by monarchs (Henry VIII), revolutionaries (Che Guevara), and even ancient peoples—remnants of archaic felted wool models have been found predating Etruscan and Minoan times. Talk about enduring fashion influence! My contribution to this tradition is Bohème (page 42), which can be easily whipped up on a whim, with snappy cables and crunchy seed-stitch texture.

I hope you enjoy making up your own versions of these historically influenced *chapeaux* and *toques*!

About 22" (56 cm) head circumference, tied, and about 11" (28) wide in lace section.

YARN

Worsted weight (#4 Medium).

SHOWN HERE: Berroco Glint (80% cotton, 12% nylon, 8% metallic; 141 yd [129 m]/50 g); #2940 Alexander (olive), 2 skeins.

NEEDLES

Size U.S. 7 (4.5 mm): straight or 16" (40 cm) circular (cir).

Adjust needle size if necessary to obtain the correct gauge.

NOTIONS

Smooth cotton waste yarn for provisional cast-on; markers (m); removable markers; stitch holders; tapestry needle.

GAUGE

21 sts and 24 rows = 4" (10 cm) in patt from Leaf chart.

jasmin
HEADSCARF

The twining green leaves of the night-blooming jasmine (*Jasminum sambac*) provided the inspiration for this easy-to-wear headwrap. The verdantly colored lightweight yarn with burnished metallic accents harkens back to the bohemian sentiments of the 1970s. I have had a secret love affair with jasmine since my very first trip to France. Never having smelled the real thing (save for the so-called jasmine incense of my college days), I thought it a cloyingly sweet scent used in copious doses by powdered *grande dames*. I was so very mistaken.

My epiphany arrived one warm summer night in a mountain village near the Pyrenees. As evening fell, the valley below was awash with birdcalls and wailing dogs; smoke from the chimney-tops signaled the arrival of autumn, and a touch of briny air rose from the sea beyond the hills. Being a flower lover and novice perfumer, I noticed a creamy, sensual, and divine scent floating above all the others. I had been unaware that I was literally surrounded by a blanket of jasmine clinging to the rough wall behind the small stone bench where I sat; only the magic of night unlocked the fragile perfume of the flowers. I have since tried to capture that experience in a bottle and now fill my days not only with playing with fiber, but the blissful enterprise of crafting artisan organic perfume and skincare concoctions (available at etsy.com/shop/FrenchGirlOrganics), many of which include the transcendent and sultry jasmine.

first half

LEAF LACE SECTION

With waste yarn and using a provisional method (see Glossary), CO 58 sts. Work the WS set-up row of Leaf chart once, then rep Rows 1–12 four times (do not rep the set-up row), then work Rows 1–3 once more, ending with a RS row—52 chart rows completed; piece measures about 8¾" (22 cm) from CO. Cut yarn, leaving a 24" (61 cm) tail for grafting. Place sts on holder.

TIE

Carefully remove waste yarn from provisional CO and place 58 live sts on needle. Join yarn with RS facing, ready to begin with a RS row.

ROW 1: (RS) Knit, correcting any st mounts if necessary.

ROW 2: (WS) [P2tog, yo] 14 times, k2tog, [yo, p2tog] 14 times—57 sts rem.

ROW 3: Knit.

ROW 4: [P2tog] 14 times, k1, [p2tog] 14 times—29 sts rem.

ROW 5: K2, [k2tog] 6 times, k1, [k2tog] 6 times, k2—17 sts rem.

ROW 6: [P2tog, yo] 4 times, k1, [yo, p2tog] 4 times.

ROW 7: Knit.

Rep Rows 6 and 7 fourteen more times, then work WS Row 6 once more—tie measures about 6" (15 cm) from last row of Leaf chart.

Dec for tip as foll:

ROW 1: (RS) [Ssk] 2 times, k9, [k2tog] 2 times—13 sts rem.

ROW 2: (WS) [P2tog, yo] 3 times, k1, [yo, p2tog] 3 times.

ROW 3: [Ssk] 2 times, k5, [k2tog] 2 times—9 sts rem.

ROW 4: [P2tog, yo] 2 times, k1, [yo, p2tog] 2 times.

ROW 5: [Ssk] 2 times, k1, [k2tog] 2 times—5 sts rem.

ROW 6: P2tog, yo, k1, yo, p2tog.

ROW 7: Ssk, k1, k2tog—3 sts rem.

ROW 8: P3tog—1 st rem; tie measures about 7½" (19 cm) from last row of Leaf chart.

Cut yarn and fasten off rem st.

LEAF

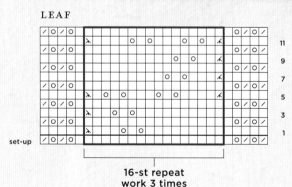

16-st repeat
work 3 times

	knit on RS; purl on WS
O	yo
/	p2tog on WS
⋏	k3tog
⅄	sssk (see Glossary)
	pattern repeat

second half

Work lace section and tie as for first half—58 live sts rem on holder.

finishing

Temporarily pin the live sts at the ends of the two halves tog and try on for fit. If necessary, adjust the length by adding or removing the same number of rows in each half, making sure to end each piece with a RS row. Every 2 rows added or removed in both halves (4 rows total) will lengthen or shorten the entire headwrap by about ¾" (2 cm). With yarn threaded on a tapestry needle, use the Kitchener st for St st (see Glossary) to graft the sts tog, taking care to include the yarnovers in each side border.

Weave in loose ends. Wet-block (see Glossary) to measurements.

FINISHED SIZE

About 19½" (49.5 cm) head circumference; see Notes.

YARN

DK weight (#3 Light).

SHOWN HERE: Shibui Baby Alpaca DK (100% baby alpaca; 255 yd [233 m]/100 g): #2001 abyss (black), 1 skein.

NEEDLES

Size U.S. 5 (3.75 mm): two 16" (40 cm) or 24" (60 cm) circular (cir).

Adjust needle size if necessary to obtain the correct gauge.

NOTIONS

Markers (m); removable markers; 12" (30.5 cm) of 1¼" (3.2 cm) wide velvet ribbon; tapestry needle; sharp-point sewing needle and matching thread for attaching ribbon; decorative brooch or pin.

GAUGE

21½ sts and 31 rnds = 4" (10 cm) in St st, worked in rnds.

sapphire
TOQUE

Looking at Sapphire, one might think this ultra-soft, luxurious baby alpaca cap was dreamed up as a romantic homage to the alluring cloches of the 1930s. Truth be told, the road to its creation was markedly circuitous. It began when I saw river eel on the menu of a waterside café in the Loire Valley of France. Surrounded by the ocean and bay most of my life, I'd never lived near a river until our thirteen-year stint in heartland Wisconsin, where, on the banks of the Fox, the ghosts of those early *voyageurs*, Marquette and Joliet, still lingered. So intriguing was this to me, with my French-Canadian roots, that I studied every aspect of their culture, from the songs they sang while navigating the rivers to the garments they wore as they labored and made merry. The smart toque that was in fashion among them was a practical, yet stylish, adaptation of the rakish "liberty cap" worn by partisans in Revolutionary-era France. My own forefathers, the Barrilleau brothers, left the motherland in the throes of those fractious times making for the shores of New France. I was thinking about them while I waited for my dinner to arrive, and feeling quite inspired by the adventure of trying some ancestral fare, I made a sketch on a tiny napkin—a tall cap anchored on one side by a wide ribbon secured with a feathered brooch. (P.S. The eels were delightful!)

notes

The baby alpaca yarn used here has some stretch to it, so this hat is sized with about 1" to 2" (2.5 to 5 cm) of negative ease to fit head circumferences of 20½" to 21½" (52 to 54.5 cm).

Yarnovers are a great alternative to wrapping stitches at short-row turning points. The yarnovers are easy to identify, and you simply work each yarnover together with the stitch next to it to close up the gaps.

For instant vintage appeal, add an antique brooch. As a stand-in, glue a pin-type closure (found in bead shops) to the back of a lovely button.

hat

Using the invisible method and substituting a second cir needle for the waste yarn (see sidebar at right), CO 104 sts. Place marker (pm) and join for working in rnds, being careful not to twist sts.

FOLDED HEM

Knit 12 rnds. Fold fabric in half with WS touching and RS facing outward to bring the working needle and the CO needle tog and parallel and so that the CO needle is in back.

HEM RND: *Insert right needle tip into the first st on each needle and work them together as k2tog; rep from * to end of rnd—104 sts on working needle; folded hem measures about ¾" (2 cm) high.

BODY

Work even in St st until piece measures 9½" (24 cm) from hem fold line.

CROWN

Place two removable markers on the needle, each 22 sts from the end-of-rnd m—44 center back sts between removable markers with end-of-rnd m in center. Work yarnover short-rows (see Notes) to shape the asymmetrical crown over the 60 center front sts as foll:

SHORT-ROW 1: (RS) Knit to first removable m, sl m, yo, knit to second removable m, turn work.

SHORT-ROW 2: (WS) Yo, purl to removable m, turn work—1 yo next to removable m at each side.

SHORT-ROW 3: Yo, knit to 3 sts before yo of previous short-row, turn work.

SHORT-ROW 4: Yo, purl to 3 sts before yo of previous short-row, turn work.

SHORT-ROWS 5–16: Rep the last 2 rows 6 more times—8 yo gaps on each side of marked section.

NEXT ROW: (RS) Yo, knit to end-of-rnd m, working each yo tog with the st after it as k2tog.

NEXT RND: Discarding removable markers as you come to them, knit all sts, working each rem yo tog with the st before it as ssk (see Glossary)—104 sts.

INVISIBLE CAST-ON USING THE CABLE OF CIRCULAR NEEDLE

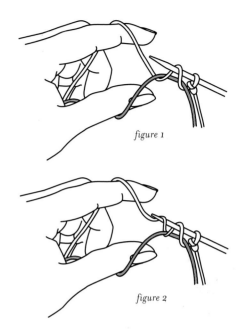

figure 1

figure 2

I like to use the cable portion of a second circular needle instead of waste yarn when working an invisible provisional cast-on. In so doing, there is no need for waste yarn, and the provisional stitches are already on a needle, ready to be worked.

To work this type of cast-on, you'll need two circular needles of the same size—two size U.S. 4 (3.5 mm) needles, for example.

Make a loose slipknot of working yarn and place it on the tip of a circular needle held in your right hand. The slipknot does not count as a stitch.

Hold the cable portion of the second needle (shaded dark) next to the slip-knot on the first needle and hold the working yarn over your left index finger.

*Bring the working needle forward under the cable, over the working yarn, grab a loop of working yarn (Figure 1), then bring the needle back behind the working yarn and grab a second loop (Figure 2)—2 stitches formed each on working needle and cable.

Repeat from * for the desired number of stitches, always adding stitches in pairs.

Continue working on the stitches on the working needle as desired, holding the provisional loops on the cable of the second needle all the while.

When you're ready to work in the opposite direction, join yarn, slide the stitches from the cable to the tip of the second needle, and work as usual, correcting the stitch mount (so the leading leg is on the front of the needle) if necessary.

You can also use this method for toe-up socks worked with one long circular needle in the magic-loop method as follows:

Make a loose slipknot of working yarn and place it on the right needle tip, about an inch from where the cable joins the tip.

Fold the cable in half and hold the tips parallel with the needle holding the slipknot on top, then pull out the lower needle tip and a length of cable.

Continue as described above for the desired number of stitches.

Continue to knit all stitches in rounds as specified in the pattern.

BUTTONHOLE RND: K49, BO 6 sts, knit to end.

NEXT RND: Knit to buttonhole gap of previous rnd, turn work so WS is facing, use the cable method (see Glossary) to CO 6 sts over buttonhole gap, turn work so RS is facing, knit to end—piece measures about 12″ (30.5 cm) from hem fold line at highest point.

Dec as foll:

RND 1: *Ssk, k11; rep from *—96 sts rem.

EVEN-NUMBERED RNDS 2–22: Knit.

RND 3: *Ssk, k10; rep from *—88 sts rem.

RND 5: *Ssk, k9; rep from *—80 sts rem.

RND 7: *Ssk, k8; rep from *—72 sts rem.

RND 9: *Ssk, k7; rep from *—64 sts rem.

RND 11: *Ssk, k6; rep from *—56 sts rem.

RND 13: *Ssk, k5; rep from *—48 sts rem.

RND 15: *Ssk, k4; rep from *—40 sts rem.

RND 17: *Ssk, k3; rep from *—32 sts rem.

RND 19: *Ssk, k2; rep from *—24 sts rem.

RND 21: *Ssk, k1; rep from *—16 sts rem.

RND 23: [Ssk] 8 times—8 sts rem.

finishing

Cut yarn, leaving a 10″ (25.5 cm) tail. Thread tail on a tapestry needle, draw through all sts, pull tight to close hole, and fasten off on WS.

Weave in loose ends. Wet-block (see Glossary), being careful not to stretch the fabric.

Thread ribbon through buttonhole and gather the fabric into gentle pleats so that about 5½″ (14 cm) of ribbon shows on the outside. Trim excess ribbon if necessary and, with sewing needle and thread, sew raw edges of ribbon tog on WS of hat. Tack the ribbon to the inside of the hat so the ribbon seam does not migrate to the outside.

Attach brooch or decorative pin.

FINISHED SIZE

About 21½" (54.5 cm) head circumference.

YARN

Chunky weight (#5 Bulky).

SHOWN HERE: Rowan Cocoon (80% merino, 20% kid mohair; 126 yd [115 m]/100 g); #802 alpine, 2 balls.

NEEDLES

HAT BODY: size U.S. 10 (6.5 mm).

RIBBING: size U.S. 9 (6 mm): 16" (40 cm) circular (cir) or set of 4 or 5 double-pointed (dpn).

Adjust needle size if necessary to obtain the correct gauge.

NOTIONS

Smooth cotton waste yarn for provisional cast-on and stitch holder; markers (m); cable needle (cn); tapestry needle.

GAUGE

10½ sts and 31 rows = 4" (10 cm) in brioche st on larger needles.

14 sts of cable panel measure 2½" (6.5 cm) at widest point on larger needles.

coquille
TOQUE

For Coquille, a cushy brioche stitch meets an equally cozy merino-mohair yarn in a re-imagination of a swirling seashell—very much like the humble bivalve of the genus *ostrea* that was its inspiration. As an oyster farmer's daughter, I know a thing or two about a good oyster and the rugged shells it lies within; my beachfront home afforded me the chance to observe oysters in detail with their fascinating crenulated ridges of overlapping mica-flecked armor protecting the coveted gem—what a contrast in textures!

In Languedoc-Roussillon, the region of Mediterranean France we visit every year with our tours, there is a small bay where the crisp waters of a mountain-born river mingle with the vast sea. The shores of the Etang de Thau are ringed with myriad *commerces de coquillages* and the luscious vineyards that produce the exceptionally delicious white wine (*Picpoul de Pinet*) that marries so well with these fruits of the Mediterranean. There, within roughly 50 square kilometers, the confluence of sun, soil, and sea has produced this happy pairing. Whenever I am in the neighborhood, I slurp down both oysters and wine with abandon.

It is also a happy event when your yarn and intended design come together in perfect alignment. Rowan Cocoon and brioche stitch are a marriage made in knitter's heaven and will reward you with a slouchy toque with meandering openwork cables and quick-to-finish construction that belies the complexity of its appearance.

notes

The twisted, asymmetrical shape results from grafting several picked-up stitches from one selvedge to a single stitch picked up from the other selvedge, instead of grafting the stitches one-for-one in the usual manner.

The flare at the base of the openwork cable panel provides a lovely curve to the brim.

Proper gauge is important for creating the right amount of drape. Make a generous swatch, large enough to determine if the effect is correct, neither too loose nor too tight.

stitch guide

Half Brioche Stitch (worked on a odd number of sts)

ROW 1: (RS) *Knit into st below st on the left needle tip and slip the st from left needle, k1; rep from * to last st, knit into st below st on left needle and slip the st from left needle.

ROW 2: (WS) Knit.

ROW 3: *K1, knit into st below st on left needle and slip st from left needle; rep from * to last st, k1.

ROW 4: Knit.

Rep Rows 1–4 for patt.

14-st Rib Cable: Sl 6 sts onto cable needle (cn) and hold in front of work, [k2, p2] 2 times, then work 6 sts from cn as k2, p2, k2.

NOTE: *When you work the first 8 cable sts you will not be knitting the purls and purling the knits as they appear; this is necessary to maintain a k2 column at each side of the cable.*

Cable Panel (worked over 14 sts)

ROWS 1, 3, 5, AND 7: (RS) [K2, p2tog, yo] 3 times, k2.

EVEN-NUMBERED ROWS 2–18: (WS) [P2, k2] 3 times, p2.

ROWS 9: Work 14-st rib cable (see above).

ROWS 11, 13, AND 15: Rep Row 1.

ROW 17: Rep Row 9.

ROW 19: Rep Row 1.

ROW 20: Rep Row 2.

Rep Rows 1–20 for patt.

hat

With larger needles, waste yarn, and using a provisional method (see Glossary), CO 64 sts. Change to main yarn and knit 1 WS row.

NEXT ROW: (RS) Work Row 1 of half brioche st (see Stitch Guide) over 37 sts, place marker (pm), work Row 1 of cable panel (see Stitch Guide) over 14 sts, pm, work Row 1 of half brioche st over rem 13 sts.

Cont in established patts until Rows 1–20 of cable panel have been worked 4 times, then work cable panel Rows 1–5 once more, ending with a RS row and removing markers as you come to them in last row—86 rows total; piece measures about 11" (28 cm) from CO. Place sts on waste yarn holder. Do not cut yarn.

gathered grafting

With larger needle, RS still facing, and beg at top of hat, pick up and knit 50 sts evenly spaced along left selvedge to bottom of hat. Cut yarn, but leave sts on needle. Hold piece with RS facing and rem selvedge running across the top and join yarn to corner at right-hand side. With other larger needle, RS facing, at beg at bottom of hat, pick up and knit 50 sts evenly along rem selvedge to top of hat. Cut yarn, leaving a 24" (61 cm) tail for grafting, and leave sts on needle.

Rearrange the sts as necessary so the tip of each needle is at the top of the hat. Hold the two needles tog and parallel with WS of fabric touching, RS facing out, and with both needle tips pointing to the right. Thread 24" (61 cm) tail on a tapestry needle. Beg at top of hat and working downward, work gathered Kitchener st to join more front sts than back sts as foll:

STEP 1: Bring threaded needle through the first st on the front needle knitwise (kwise), pull the yarn through, and slip this st off the needle—1 st removed from front needle.

STEP 2: Bring threaded needle through the next 3 sts on the front needle pwise, pull the yarn through, and leave these sts on the needle.

STEP 3: Bring threaded needle through the first st on the back needle pwise, pull the yarn through, and slip this st off the needle—1 st removed from back needle.

STEP 4: Bring threaded needle through the next st on the back needle kwise, pull the yarn through, and leave this st on the needle.

STEP 5: Bring threaded needle through the first 3 sts on the front needle kwise, pull the yarn through, and slip these sts off the needle—3 sts removed from front needle.

STEP 6: Bring threaded needle through the next 3 sts on the front needle pwise, pull the yarn through, and leave these sts on the needle.

STEPS 7 AND 8: Rep Steps 3 and 4—1 st removed from back needle.

Repeat Steps 5–8 only 7 more times—25 sts on front needle and 41 sts on back needle rem.

Prepare for working regular Kitchener st as foll:

STEP 1: Bring threaded needle through the first 3 sts on the front needle kwise, pull the yarn through, and slip these sts off the needle—3 sts removed from front needle.

STEP 2: Bring threaded needle through the next st on the front needle pwise, pull the yarn through, and leave this st on the needle.

STEP 3: Bring threaded needle through the first st on the back needle pwise, pull the yarn through, and slip this st off the needle—1 st removed from back needle.

STEP 4: Bring threaded needle through the next st on the back needle kwise, pull the yarn through, and leave this st on the needle—22 sts on front needle and 40 sts on back needle rem.

Work regular Kitchener st for St st (see Glossary) to join next 10 sts on each needle one-for-one—12 sts on front needle and 30 sts on back needle rem.

Cont in gathered Kitchener st to join more back sts than front sts as foll:

STEP 1: Bring threaded needle through the first st on the front needle kwise, pull the yarn through, and slip this st off the needle—1 st removed from front needle.

STEP 2: Bring threaded needle through the next st on the front needle pwise, pull the yarn through, and leave this st on the needle.

STEP 3: Bring threaded needle through the first st on the back needle pwise, pull the yarn through, and slip this st off the needle—1 st removed from back needle.

STEP 4: Bring threaded needle through the next 4 sts on the back needle kwise, pull the yarn through, and leave these sts on the needle.

STEPS 5 AND 6: Rep Steps 1 and 2—1 st removed from front needle.

STEP 7: Bring threaded through needle the first 4 sts on the back needle pwise, pull the yarn through, and slip these sts off the needle—4 sts removed from back needle.

STEP 8: Bring threaded needle through the next 4 sts on the back needle kwise, pull the yarn through, and leave these sts on needle.

Rep Steps 5–8 only 4 more times—6 sts rem on front needle, 9 sts rem on back needle.

Transition to regular Kitchener st again as foll:

STEP 1: Bring threaded needle through the first st on the front needle kwise, pull the yarn through, and slip this st off the needle—1 st removed from front needle.

STEP 2: Bring threaded needle through the next st on the front needle pwise, pull the yarn through, and leave this st on the needle.

STEP 3: Bring threaded needle the first 4 sts on the back needle pwise, pull the yarn through, and slip these sts off the needle—4 sts removed from back needle.

STEP 4: Bring threaded needle through the next st on the back needle kwise, pull the yarn through, and leave this st on needle—5 sts rem on each needle.

Work regular Kitchener st for St st to join rem sts one-for-one.

finishing

With tail threaded on a tapestry needle, draw yarn through the 64 live sts on waste yarn holder at top of hat, pull tight to gather and close top of hat. Fasten off yarn on WS, using tails to close up any holes.

RIBBING

Carefully remove waste yarn from provisional CO and place 64 live sts on smaller cir needle or dpn. Pm and join for working in rnds. With RS facing, work rib as foll, correcting st mount of CO sts, if necessary, as you work:

RND 1: [K1, p1] 6 times, k1, p2tog, [k2, yo, p2tog] 3 times, k2, p1, [k1, p1] 17 times—63 sts.

RND 2: [K1, p1] 7 times, [k2, p2] 3 times, k2, p1, [k1, p1] 17 times.

RND 3: [K1, p1] 7 times, [k2, yo, p2tog] 3 times, k2, p1, [k1, p1] 17 times.

Rep Rnds 2 and 3 once more—ribbing measures about 1" (2.5 cm).

Using Jeny's Surprisingly Stretchy method (see Glossary), BO all sts.

Weave in loose ends. Block if desired.

FINISHED SIZE

About 21" (53.5 cm) head circumference, after blocking.

YARN

Worsted weight (#4 Medium).

SHOWN HERE: Berroco Lustra (50% wool, 50% Tencel; 197 yd [180 m]/100 g); #3165 kir (red), 1 skein.

NEEDLES

HAT: size U.S. 7 (4.5 mm): set of 4 or 5 double-pointed (dpn) or two 24" (60 cm) or one 40" (100 cm) circular (cir), depending on your chosen method for working in the rnd.

EARFLAPS: size U.S. 8 (5 mm).

Adjust needle size if necessary to obtain the correct gauge.

NOTIONS

Marker (m); stitch holders; cardboard for making tassels; tapestry needle.

GAUGE

1 patt rep (16 to 18 sts) from Rnds 66–81 of Tulip chart measures 5¼" (13.5 cm) wide on smaller needles, after blocking.

31 rnds of Tulip chart measure = 4" (10 cm) on smaller needles, after blocking (see Notes).

tulipe
CAP

Tulipe was the first piece I designed for this book, and it quite nearly became the last I ever knitted. I began with the well-known snowdrops lace stitch and endeavored to knit the hat organically from the flower-like crown medallion, freestyling the ensuing lace with yarnovers and decreases. The fact that it took almost two years to knit is another tale.

As many of you know, I am a *cuisinière* (otherwise dubbed *foodie*) and have experimented in the kitchen since the age of ten. I had recently acquired the Cadillac of stick-blenders (the culinary-obsessed will understand)—a shiny, powerful little machine that can whip up a disparate assortment of soup-pot inhabitants into the most velvety purée that ever touched your lips. My *velouté de champignons* (creamy mushroom bisque) was a hit and the company well fed. My downfall was in not unplugging said blender as I assiduously scrubbed the inner blades while gripping the handle dangerously near the "on" button. The result: one trip to the emergency room with hand encased in a bag of frozen peas, fourteen sutures, two doses of painkiller, and one very grateful designer who thanked her lucky stars that she had a finger left to knit (and cook) with. Tulipe was ultimately resurrected and regained her composure, as did I, and the rest, they say, is history.

notes

For a slightly larger or smaller hat, use larger or smaller needles.

The sample hat was blocked aggressively to open up the lace pattern and gained about 2" (5 cm) in length compared to its pre-blocking length.

The blocked gauge is deliberately looser and more open than the stockinette gauge suggested on the yarn label.

If you decide to substitute a different yarn, work a generous swatch, block it, and evaluate whether it will create the same effect as the yarn shown.

stitch guide

K1b-inc: Insert right needle tip from front to back into the purl "bump" of the stitch below the next stitch on the left needle, lift the bump onto the left needle and knit it through the back loop, then knit the next stitch on the left needle as usual—1 st inc'd.

hat

With smaller needles and using Emily Ocker's circular method (see Glossary), CO 8 sts. Arrange sts on 3 or 4 dpn, two 24" (60 cm) cir needles, or one 40" (100 cm) cir needle for magic-loop method, place marker (pm), and join for working in rnds, being careful not to twist sts. Rnds beg at center back.

RND 1: Knit.

RND 2: [K1f&b (see Glossary)] 8 times—16 sts.

RND 3: [K1b-inc (see Stitch Guide), k1] 8 times—24 sts.

RND 4: [K1b-inc, k2] 12 times—32 sts.

RND 5: Knit.

RNDS 6–64: Work in patt from Tulip chart, working chart patt 4 times for each rnd and inc as shown—72 sts after Rnd 64.

RND 65: Remove end-of-rnd m, return last st worked to left needle tip, replace m—end-of-rnd m has moved 1 st to the right. Work Rnd 65 of chart, ending at new m position.

RNDS 66–76: Work in patt from chart—64 sts rem after Rnd 76.

RND 77: Rep Rnd 65—end-of-rnd m has moved 1 st to the right.

RNDS 78–81: Work in patt from chart—72 sts rem after Rnd 81.

RIBBING

RND 1: *K2, yo, p2tog; rep from *.

RNDS 2 AND 4: *K2, p2; rep from *.

RND 3: *K2, p2tog, yo; rep from *.

RND 5: Working in established k2, p2 rib patt, BO 7 sts for half of back, work in patt until there are 13 sts on right needle after BO gap, place 13 sts just worked on holder for earflap, BO next 32 sts for front of hat, work in patt until there are 13 sts after second BO gap and place these sts on holder for other earflap, BO rem 7 sts for other half of back—2 groups of 13 sts each rem on holders for earflaps.

☐	knit
⊙	yo
╱	k2tog
╲	ssk
⋀	sl 2 as if to k2tog, k1, p2sso
⋔	k4tog
▓	no stitch
☐	pattern repeat

TULIP RNDS 6–43

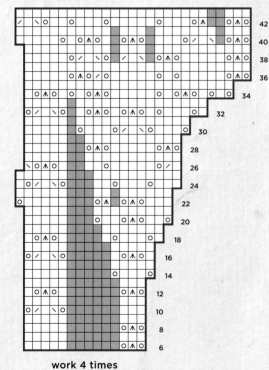

work 4 times

*See instructions.

TULIP RNDS 44–81

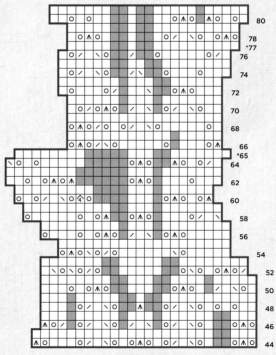

work 4 times

*See instructions.

EARFLAPS

Place 13 held sts for one earflap on larger needles and join yarn with RS facing. Work back and forth in rows as foll:

ROW 1: (RS) K2tog, [k2tog, yo] 4 times, k1, k2tog—11 sts rem.

EVEN-NUMBERED ROWS 2–12: (WS) Sl 1 pwise with yarn in front (wyf), purl to end.

ROW 3: Ssk, yo, k7, yo, k2tog.

ROW 5: Sl 1 pwise with yarn in back (wyb), k1, yo, ssk, k3, k2tog, yo, k2.

ROW 7: Sl 1 pwise wyb, ssk, yo, ssk, k1, k2tog, yo, k2tog, k1—9 sts rem.

ROW 9: Sl 1 pwise wyb, ssk, yo, sl 2 tog knitwise, k1, p2sso, yo, k2tog, k1—7 sts rem.

ROW 11: Sl 1 pwise wyb, ssk, yo, k1, yo, k2tog, k1.

ROW 13: Sl 1 pwise wyb, ssk, k1, k2tog, k1—5 sts rem.

ROW 14: Sl 1 pwise wyb, p3tog, p1—3 sts rem.

ROW 15: K3tog—1 st rem.

Cut yarn leaving a 16" (40.5 cm) tail and draw tail through rem st.

Work the second earflap in the same manner.

finishing

TIES

For each tie, cut three 32" (81.5 cm) strands of yarn. Thread all three strands on a tapestry needle and draw them halfway through the BO loop at tip of earflap—seven strands total, including earflap tail. Divide into two outer groups of two strands each and an inner group of three strands, then braid the three groups for about 12" (30.5 cm). Secure the end of the braid with an overhand knot.

TASSELS

Cut cardboard about 4" (10 cm) wide and 3" (7.5 cm) high. Make two tassels 3" (7.5 cm) tall (see Glossary), winding the yarn 14 times around the cardboard for each tassel, and leaving long tails at the top. Use the long tails to attach tassels to ends of ties as shown.

Wet-block (see Glossary) to about 10½" (26.5 cm) across at the lower edge (21" [53.5 cm] circumference) and about 11" (28 cm) tall from CO to end of ribbing (see Notes), not counting earflaps. Block earflaps to about 3" (7.5 cm) long, not including the ties.

Weave in loose ends.

FINISHED SIZE

About 19¼" (49 cm) head circumference.

Note: hat is deliberately close-fitting.

YARN

Sportweight (#2 Fine).

SHOWN HERE: Quince & Co. Sparrow (100% linen; 168 yd [154 m]/50 g): natural (A), 1 skein.

Rowan Classic Siena (100% mercerized cotton; 153 yd [140 m]/50 g): black (B), 1 skein.

NEEDLES

HAT: size U.S. 2 (2.75 mm): 16" (40 cm) circular (cir) and set of 4 or 5 double-pointed (dpn).

EDGING: size U.S. 3 (3.25 mm): 16" (40 cm) cir.

Adjust needle size if necessary to obtain the correct gauge.

NOTIONS

Markers (m); tapestry needle.

GAUGE

21 sts and 39 rnds = 4" (10 cm) in St st, worked in rnds on smaller needle.

tartine

STRIPED CAP

There was a small café perched along a roughly paved alleyway in the 2nd arrondissement of Paris where I ate my first tartine. Sure, you can say it is nothing more than a glorified hunk of baguette smeared with Nutella or *confiture*, but it marked a red-letter day in France—the national election between Sarkozy and his challenger, one (very socialist) Ségolène Royal—so it has remained quite memorable.

A cobblestone's throw from the more storied monuments, this remains a very much workaday neighborhood with a glorious market street far from the tourist-ed eyes of best-selling guidebook worshipers. Madame Royal's campaign headquarters was, of course, centered in this bohemian stronghold, and *après-tartine* we slipped in to view the returns with her loyalists on a makeshift visual feed. Madame went down to defeat . . . yet other than that, I recall only my tartine.

Basic to French life, tartine is an after-school treat, all crunchy and layered with delicious toppings . . . what more fitting name for this cheerfully striped *chapeau*? Perhaps it was the chocolate-hued Nutella and pale slivers of crisp bread that inspired the color palette, or perhaps it was the deeply inky *confiture de figues* and the mounds of Normandy butter. Whatever the provenance, you'll find this cotton-linen cloche satisfying and easy to knit, with a hint of Gallic flair that is very much like a tartine—just right.

notes

Add or remove 4-round stripes as necessary to adjust the size; every 4 rounds more or fewer will lengthen or shorten the hat by about ½" (1.3 cm).

There is no need to cut yarn at the color changes. Carry the unused color up along the wrong side of the work until it is needed again and twist the colors together every few rounds to keep the inside of the hat tidy.

To work stripes in the round without a "jog" at the start of a new color, twist the yarns together first, remove the end-of-round marker, slip the first stitch of the old round, replace the marker, and continue with the new color. On the following round, knit all stitches (including the slipped stitch) with the new color.

hat

EDGING

With A and larger needle, CO 123 sts. Do not join. Work the first rnd as a RS row, then join at the end of the row as foll:

RND 1: Sl 1 purlwise with yarn in back, k1, yo, *k5, slip the second, third, fourth, and fifth st on the right needle tip over the first st and off the needle, yo; rep from * to last st, bring ends of rnd tog, being careful not to twist sts, and work the last st tog with the slipped first st as k2tog to join for working in rnds, place marker (pm)—51 sts rem.

RND 2: K1, *work [p1 through back loop (tbl), yo, k1] all in next st, k1; rep from *—101 sts.

RND 3: K2, k1tbl, *k3, k1tbl; rep from * to last 2 sts, k2.

Knit 3 rnds even—piece measures about ⅝" (1.6 cm) from CO.

BODY

Change to smaller needle and join B. [Knit 4 rnds B, knit 4 rnds A] 9 times (see Notes for changing colors), then knit 4 rnds B—76 rnds total; 19 four-rnd stripes completed; piece measures about 8½" (21.5 cm) from CO (see Notes for customizing length).

CROWN

Cont in St st stripes as established, changing to dpn when sts no longer fit comfortably on cir needle, as foll:

RND 1: With A, knit.

RND 2: With A, [ssk, k8] 9 times, ssk, k9—91 sts rem.

RND 3: With A, knit.

RND 4: With A, [ssk, k7] 9 times, ssk, k8—81 sts rem.

RND 5: With B, [ssk, k6] 9 times, ssk, k7—71 sts rem.

RND 6: With B, knit.

RND 7: With B, [ssk, k5] 9 times, ssk, k6—61 sts rem.

RND 8: With B, knit.

RND 9: With A, [ssk, k4] 9 times, ssk, k5—51 sts rem.

RND 10: With A, knit.

RND 11: With A, [ssk, k3] 9 times, ssk, k4—41 sts rem.

RND 12: With A, knit.

RND 13: With B, [ssk, k2] 9 times, ssk, k3—31 sts rem.

RND 14: With B, knit.

RND 15: With B, [ssk, k1] 9 times, ssk, k2—21 sts rem.

RND 16: With B, [ssk] 10 times, k1—11 sts rem; piece measures about 10¼" (26 cm) from CO.

finishing

Cut yarn, leaving a 10" (25.5 cm) tail. Thread tail on tapestry needle, draw through rem sts, pull tight to close hole, and fasten off on WS.

Weave in loose ends.

Wet-block (see Glossary), slightly flaring out the brim as shown and stretching as necessary to fit head.

TWISTED TIE

Cut two strands of B, each 80" (203 cm) long. Tie strands tog at one end in an overhand knot. Loop knotted end over a doorknob and, holding one strand in each hand, make a twisted cord (see Glossary) about 36" (91.5 cm) long. Tie an overhand knot near the other end of cord and trim both ends. Thread cord through eyelets in edging and tie in a loose bow as shown.

FINISHED SIZE

About 22" (56 cm) head circumference.

YARN

Chunky weight (#5 Bulky).

SHOWN HERE: Rowan Big Wool (100% merino; 87 yd [80 m]/100 g): #048 linen, 2 balls.

NEEDLES

RIBBING: size U.S. 11 (8 mm): 16" (40 cm) circular (cir).

BODY: size U.S. 15 (10 mm): 16" (40 cm) and set of 4 or 5 double-pointed (dpn).

Adjust needle size if necessary to obtain the correct gauge.

NOTIONS

Markers (m); removable markers; stitch holders; cable needle (cn); tapestry needle.

GAUGE

$11\frac{1}{2}$ sts = 4" (10 cm) in k2, p2 rib on smaller cir needle.

10 sts and 14 rnds = 4" (10 cm) in seed st on larger cir needle, worked in rnds.

6 sts of 3/3LC cable measure about $1\frac{3}{4}$" (4.5 cm) wide on larger cir needle.

bohème

BERET

Back in the day when I adored the Beatles, I was desperately envious of, and infinitely inspired by, any woman that was on George Harrison's arm. My muse (and his, too, I suppose) was the doubly hip and classy Pattie Boyd, now a brilliant photographer and most infamously the subject of Eric Clapton's longingly beautiful song, "Layla." It was a snapshot of the stylin' Ms. Boyd, complete with a large-scale crocheted tam perched fetchingly askew that has been stuck in my mind for these many years. As much as I am enraptured by that era, the yarn choices were pitiful at the time, and the thought of creating my perfect beret with the hideously garish offerings from the local dime store left me hatless.

My patience paid off and now, more than thirty years later, I found my dreamed-of hat in Bohème (one of my favorite French words beside *pamplemousse*)—an oversized beret of 1960's London sentiments paired with a diagonal Aran cable that is at once modern and decidedly vintage in feel. Rowan Big Wool worked at a relatively tight gauge gives this charmer serious street "cred" and ramps up the warmth for the chilliest outings, yet remains light and frothy due to the airy yarn construction. This design also affords you a great excuse to experiment with working cables without using a cable needle—a technique that, once learned, will free up hours of knitting time for, well, more knitting!

notes

Instead of using a 16″ (40 cm) circular needle and changing to double-pointed needles later, consider working the hat entirely on two circular needles. This is great way to deal with smaller projects that use bulky yarns.

Achieving the correct gauge in k2, p2 rib is key to achieving the correct head size. Work a sample of the ribbing in the round according to the instructions (in the sidebar on page 45).

For a less slouchy hat, increase the crown to only 84 stitches, instead of 90 stitches, and work fewer rounds as follows: Work Rnds 1–14 of the crown, then omit Rnds 15–18. For the decreases at the top of the hat, omit Rnds 1 and 2, then work from Rnd 3 to the end, adjusting the knits and purls in the seed-stitch sections as necessary to maintain the established pattern.

Big Wool and other soft merino yarns have a tendency to become felted just by looking at them! Take care to wash and rinse in cool water with no agitation, then roll gently in a towel to remove excess water.

stitch guide

3/3LC: Slip 3 sts onto cn and hold in front of work, k3, k3 from cn.

2/2LC: Slip 2 sts onto cn and hold in front of work, k2, k2 from cn.

Seed Stitch Worked in Rounds for Gauge Swatch (even number of sts)

RND 1: *K1, p1; rep from *.

RND 2: *P1, k1; rep from *.

Rep Rnds 1 and 2 for patt.

hat

BRIM

With smaller cir needle and using a provisional method (see Glossary), CO 65 sts. Do not join. Work as foll: *K2, p2; rep from * to last st, place marker (pm) for beg of rnd, bring ends of needle tog (being careful not to twist sts), work last st tog with first st as k2tog to join in the rnd, k1, p2, *k2, p2; rep from * to m and end of rnd—64 sts rem.

Work 4 more rnds even in k2, p2 rib as established.

CROWN

NOTE: *See page 46 for working cables without a cable needle.*

Change to larger cir needle. Work seed st and cable patt as foll:

RND 1: Ssk, knit into the front and back of the next st (k1f&b; see Glossary), k1, yo, 3/3LC (see Stitch Guide), *ssk, k1, p1, k1, yo, 3/3LC; rep from * to last 10 sts, ssk, k1f&b, p1, yo, 3/3LC—66 sts.

RND 2: *K1, [p1, k1] 2 times for seed st, k6 for cable; rep from *.

RND 3: *Ssk, p1, k1, p1, yo, k6; rep from*.

RND 4: *K1, [k1, p1] 2 times, k6; rep from *.

RND 5: *Ssk, k1, p1, k1f&b, yo, k6; rep from *—72 sts.

RND 6: *K1, [p1, k1] 2 times, p1, k6; rep from *.

RND 7: *Ssk, [p1, k1] 2 times, yo, 3/3LC; rep from *.

RND 8: *K1, [k1, p1] 2 times, k7; rep from *.

RND 9: *Ssk, k1, p1, k1, purl into front and back of next st (p1f&b; see Glossary), yo, k6; rep from *—78 sts.

RND 10: *K1, [p1, k1] 3 times, k6; rep from *.

RND 11: *Ssk, [p1, k1] 2 times, p1, yo, k6; rep from *.

RND 12: *K1, [k1, p1] 3 times, k6; rep from *.

RND 13: *Ssk, [k1, p1] 2 times, k1f&b, yo, 3/3LC; rep from *—84 sts.

RND 14: *K1, [p1, k1] 3 times, p1, k6; rep from *.

RND 15: *Ssk [p1, k1] 2 times, p1, k1f&b, yo, k6—90 sts.

RND 16: *K1, [k1, p1] 4 times, k6; rep from *.

RND 17: *Ssk, [k1, p1] 3 times, k1, yo, k6.

RND 18: *K1, [p1, k1] 4 times, k6; rep from*.

Dec for top of hat as foll:

RND 1: *Ssk, [p1, k1] 2 times, p1, k2tog, yo, 3/3LC; rep from *—84 sts rem.

RND 2: *K1, [k1, p1] 3 times, k7; rep from *.

RND 3: *Ssk, [k1, p1] 2 times, k2tog, yo, k6; rep from *—78 sts rem.

RND 4: *K1, [p1, k1] 3 times, k6; rep from *.

RND 5: *Ssk, p1, k1, p1, k2tog, yo, k6—72 sts rem.

RND 6: *K2, p1, k1, p2tog, k6; rep from *—66 sts rem.

RND 7: *Ssk, k1, p2tog, yo, 3/3LC—60 sts rem.

WORKING A GAUGE SWATCH FOR CIRCULAR KNITTING

Because most of us purl with slightly looser tension than we knit, gauges for circular knitting (worked in rounds) are typically a little tighter than those for flat knitting (worked in rows). If you don't want to knit a gauge swatch in the round, you can work it flat if you cast on the appropriate number of stitches for the gauge swatch onto a double-pointed or circular needle and work every row as a right-side row as follows:

ROW 1: With (RS), work the stitches in the pattern specified.

ROW 2: Slide the stitches to other tip of the needle, then *leaving enough slack in the working yarn to equal about twice the width of the piece, work the first stitch with the working yarn, then use the loose strand to work the next row of pattern.

ROW 3: Slide the stitches to the other tip of the needle, pick up working yarn that was used for the first stitch on the previous row, and work the next row of pattern across all stitches.

Repeat Rows 2 and 3 until the swatch is the desired length.

WORKING CABLES WITHOUT A CABLE NEEDLE

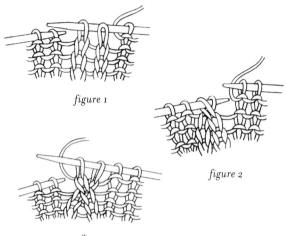

figure 1

figure 2

figure 3

STEP 1: Slip the designated number of stitches (one stitch shown) off of the left needle tip and let it rest in the front of the work for a left-leaning cable or in the back of the work for a right-leaning cable.

STEP 2: Slip the designated number of stitches (one stitch shown) onto right needle tip to temporarily hold it, keeping the resting stitch in front or back (**Figure 1**).

STEP 3: Return the resting stitch onto the left needle tip, then return the held stitch from the right needle tip onto the left tip (**Figure 2**).

STEP 4: Knit these stitches in their new order (**Figure 3**).

RND 8: *K1, p1, k2tog, k6; rep from *—54 sts rem.

RND 9: *Ssk, k2tog, yo, k5; rep from *—48 sts rem.

RND 10: *K2, k2tog, k4; rep from *—42 sts rem.

RND 11: *Ssk, k2tog, yo, k3; rep from *—36 sts rem.

RNDS 12 AND 14: Knit.

RND 13: *Ssk, yo, k2tog, k2; rep from *—30 sts rem.

RND 15: *K1, 2/2LC (see Stitch Guide); rep from *.

RND 16: *Ssk; rep from *—15 sts rem.

RND 17: *Ssk; rep from * to last st, k1—8 sts rem.

Cut yarn, leaving a 10" (25.5 cm) tail. Thread tail on tapestry needle, draw through rem sts, pull tight to close hole, and fasten off on WS.

finishing

Weave in loose ends. Wet-block (see Glossary) carefully if desired, using a dinner plate as a blocking form.

Les mitaines et les chaussettes

MITTENS AND SOCKS

HAND AND FOOT COVERINGS HAVE THEIR ROOTS IN THE DEEPEST CORNERS OF HUMAN HISTORY, from recently unearthed Bronze Age crude leather-laced slippers to the heavily decorated leggings and moccasins of the world's native peoples. The makers of the past excelled at taking something completely utilitarian and creating a thing of beauty, each stitch embedded with their cultural DNA. Thankfully, much remains for us to marvel at and learn from. Witness the artistry of Sami mittens from Upper Scandinavia, Mongol herdsmen's appliquéd leather boots, or North American Plains tribeswomen's intricately beaded gloves for a glimpse of this rich legacy.

Much of what I create springs from inspiration as varied as pre-1950 French *haute couture* to indigenous motifs, so for the two fingerless gloves and the three *chaussettes* in the following section, you will find these design elements blended and reimagined in fanciful ways. Rough-and-ready entwined Aran cables meet downy soft cashmere lace in Blanche-Neige (page 50) over-the-knee stockings. Add a distressed silk fabric tie, and the effect is a beguiling tattered elegance. Peeking into a Victorian lady's boudoir, I mused on what her lacy finely worked day gloves would become when combined with sturdy, yet silky, Italian linen yarn—the Noémie fingerless *mitaines* (page 56) were the result. These easily translate to Goth-black silk or cozy cashmere with completely distinct results.

I would be remiss if mention were not made of French and Russian ballet's contribution to the world of knitting design. The Tutu slippers (page 62) are a very deep bow to ballet's invaluable resource of design genius—the artful costumes and sets that graced everything from the Nijinsky's *Ballet Russe* to Christian Lacroix's modern take on *La Source* could enthrall one for hours. To keep your toes properly adorned, I chose a lively persimmon color for my modern Mary Jane ballet slippers to liven up those lengthy winter nights.

The adorable short Plume (page 68) socks are inspired by the fashionable footwear of the 1940s and are an elegant foil for the strapped vintage shoes I favor. Plume gives you a chance to practice intricate lace work on a very approachable scale with a super wearable result.

The Gabrielle fingerless gloves (page 74) have echoes of finely detailed Norwegian Selbu mittens with their crisp black-and-white imprint. It is no wonder this chromatic duo was taken up by Madame Chanel as the cornerstone of her design cosmos. I couldn't resist adding some cheeky oversized vintage buttons as faux closures to these easy mitts and tell myself Coco might have done the same.

The projects in this section offer a wonderful way to raid your stash or explore a new luxurious yarn . . . have a lovely time doing so!

FINISHED SIZE

About 8" (20.5 cm) foot circumference, 9½" (24 cm) foot length from back of heel to tip of toe, 10" (25.5 cm) thigh circumference unstretched, and 18½" (47 cm) leg length from top of heel to top of leg.

To fit women's U.S. shoe sizes 8–9.

YARN

Aran weight (#4 Medium) and fingering weight (#1 Super Fine).

SHOWN HERE: Rowan RYC Cashsoft Aran (57% merino, 33% microfiber, 10% cashmere; 95 yd [87 m]/ 50 g): #013 cream (MC1), 8 balls.

NOTE: *This yarn has been discontinued; suggested substitutions are Debbie Bliss Cashmerino Aran or Sublime Yarns Cashmere Merino Silk Aran.*

Rowan Kidsilk Haze (70% kid mohair, 30% silk; 229 yd [209 m]/25 g): #590 pearl (MC2), 2 balls.

Filatura di Crose Superior (70% cashmere, 30% schappe silk; 328 yd [300 m]/25 g): #01 white (CC), 1 ball.

NEEDLES

LEG AND FOOT: size U.S. 9 (5.5 mm): set of 4 or 5 double-pointed (dpn) or 40" (100 cm) or longer circular (cir) if using the magic-loop method.

EDGING: size 8 (5 mm) and size U.S. 10 (6 mm): straight.

Adjust needle size if necessary to obtain the correct gauge.

NOTIONS

Markers (m); cable needle (cn); stitch holders; tapestry needle, 2 yd (1.8 m) of ½" to ¾" (1.3 to 2 cm) silk ribbon (see Notes).

GAUGE

17 sts and 25 rnds = 4" (10 cm) in St st on size 9 (5.5 mm) needles.

20 sts of Cable chart measure 3¼" (8.5 cm) wide on size 9 (5.5 mm) needles.

7 to 11 sts of Flower chart (see Notes) measure 1¾" (4.5 cm) wide on size 9 (5.5 mm) needles.

17 sts and 16 rows = 4" (10 cm) in patt from Lace chart on size 8 (5 mm) needles, after blocking.

blanche-neige

STOCKINGS

Don't you adore the idea of being snowbound in the French Alps, curled up on a sheepskin rug with a good book tucked in your lap, a fire crackling at the hearth, and a decadent *Tartiflette* simmering in the oven? That was my fantasy as I knitted the meandering cables of Blanche-Neige (or Snow White, if you will). As the yarn traveled through my fingers, I mind-voyaged to an ice-sprinkled, gingerbread Alpine getaway with the indulgent thought of wearing these luxurious, over-the-knee *grandes chaussettes* while resting on the aforementioned woolly carpet. The French (very wisely) have a two-week mid-winter break in February when the frosty peaks are dotted with families skiing and cavorting with abandon, then ferociously downing mountains of fabulously rich traditional fare. My favorite, *Tartiflette* (layers of potatoes, crispy *lardons*, crème fraîche, and Reblochon cheese in all its extravagant glory), should only be consumed after hours of vigorous exercise (and sadly knitting does not count!).

Luckily, as knitters we can make at least part of this daydream reality. Blanche-Neige, done up in a cashmere-blend Aran-weight yarn held in tandem with a strand of kid mohair-silk and fancifully finished with an airy lace topping, is fit for any escapist, snow-filled vision you might have. Plus, they are so downright cozy, you may never want to take them off! If your taste runs a little less over-the-top, consider a shorter version sans ruffle. Try ankle or knee length with a pert 2×2 ribbing at the finish for all the comfort with less frou-frou—it's your choice.

notes

These socks are knitted with one strand each of Aran- and fingering-weight yarn held together.

Worked from the toe up, Blanche-Neige is the ultimate in versatility because you can choose to end at the ankle for an adorable bootie (with or without the lace edging) or continue up the leg for a calf, knee, or over-the-knee finish.

If you use a different Aran-weight main yarn, take care to choose one that provides good cable definition.

The stitch count of the Flower chart does not remain constant. It starts by increasing gradually from 1 to 7 sts in the first 16 rounds. After that, the main 16-round repeat varies from 7 stitches to a maximum of 11 stitches as each new flower motif begins and ends.

As an option, end the leg with k2, p2 ribbing worked to the desired length instead of the accent yarn lace edging.

The silk ribbon shown here was made by ripping lightweight silk fabric into 1" (2.5 cm) strips.

toe

With MC1 and MC2 held tog and size 9 (5.5 mm) needles, use the invisible method (see sidebar on page 23) to CO 10 sts.

NEXT RND: K10, use a separate needle to knit across 10 sts from base of provisional CO—20 sts total; 10 sts each on two needles. Rnds beg at start of instep sts.

Knit 1 rnd even.

TOE INC RND: For instep: k1, work a right-slanting lifted increase LRI (see Glossary) in next st, knit to last instep st, work LRI in next st; for sole: k1, work LRI in next st, knit to last sole st, work LRI in last st—4 sts inc'd; 2 sts each for instep and sole.

Rep the toe inc rnd every other rnd 4 more times—40 sts total: 20 sts each for instep and sole; toe measures 1½" (3.8 cm).

foot

NOTE: *After working Rnds 1–12 of Cable chart the first time, rep Rnds 13–34 for patt.*

SET-UP RND: Work Rnd 1 of Cable chart over 20 instep sts, k20 sole sts to end.

Keeping sole sts in St st, work Rnds 2–34 of chart once, then work Rnds 13–16 once more—piece measures about 7½" (19 cm) from start of toe.

gussets

NEXT RND: Work 20 instep sts in patt, k1, work LRI in each of next 2 sts, knit to last 2 sole sts, work LRI in each of next 2 sts—4 sole sts inc'd.

Work 1 rnd even.

INC RND: Work 20 instep sts in patt, k1, work LRI in next st, knit to last sole st, work LRI in last st—2 sts sole sts inc'd.

[Work 1 rnd even, rep inc rnd] 3 times, ending with Rnd 25 of chart—52 sts total: 20 instep sts, 32 sole sts; piece measures about 9" (23 cm) from start of toe.

TURN HEEL

Place 20 instep sts on holder. Work heel back and forth in short-rows on 32 sole sts as foll:

ROW 1: (RS) K18, ssk, k1, turn work.

ROW 2: (WS) Sl 1, p5, p2tog, p1, turn work.

ROW 3: Sl 1, knit to 1 st before gap formed on previous RS row, ssk (1 st each side of gap), k1, turn work.

ROW 4: Sl 1, purl to 1 st before gap formed on previous WS row, p2tog (1 st each side of gap), p1, turn work.

Rep Rows 3 and 4 until all heel sts have been worked, ending with WS Row 4 and omitting the k1 or p1 after the dec in the final 2 rows—18 sts rem. Return 20 held instep sts to needle.

JOINING RND: (Rnd 26 of Cable chart) On heel needle, sl 1, k16, ssk (last heel st tog with first instep st; on instep needle, work LRI in next instep st (counts as k2 at beg of chart), work in patt to last 2 instep sts, work LRI in next instep st (counts as k2 at end of chart), transfer last instep to heel needle; on heel needle, k2tog (last instep st tog with first heel st, knit to end of heel sts again—38 sts total; 20 instep sts for front of leg, 18 heel sts for back of leg. Rnd begins at start of front leg.

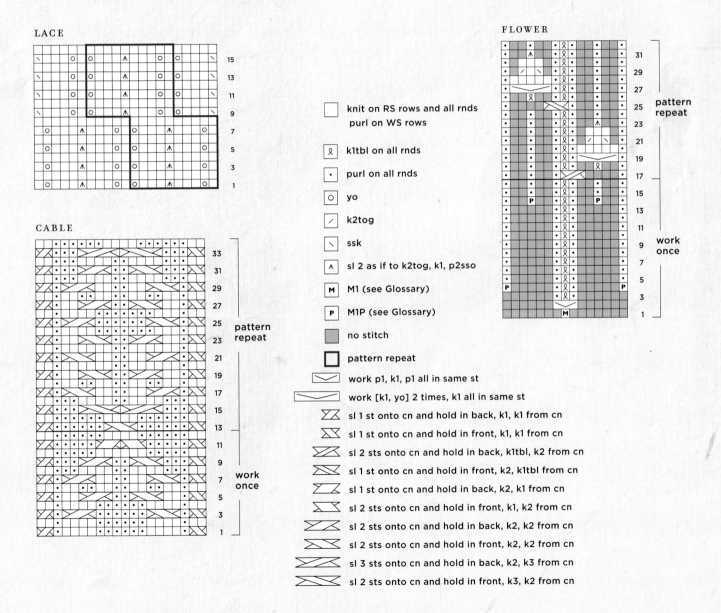

LACE

CABLE

FLOWER

pattern repeat

work once

☐ knit on RS rows and all rnds
purl on WS rows

Ⴘ k1tbl on all rnds

· purl on all rnds

O yo

/ k2tog

\ ssk

⋀ sl 2 as if to k2tog, k1, p2sso

M M1 (see Glossary)

P M1P (see Glossary)

▨ no stitch

☐ pattern repeat

⌣ work p1, k1, p1 all in same st

⌣ work [k1, yo] 2 times, k1 all in same st

sl 1 st onto cn and hold in back, k1, k1 from cn

sl 1 st onto cn and hold in front, k1, k1 from cn

sl 2 sts onto cn and hold in back, k1tbl, k2 from cn

sl 1 st onto cn and hold in front, k2, k1tbl from cn

sl 1 st onto cn and hold in back, k2, k1 from cn

sl 2 sts onto cn and hold in front, k1, k2 from cn

sl 2 sts onto cn and hold in back, k2, k2 from cn

sl 2 sts onto cn and hold in front, k2, k2 from cn

sl 3 sts onto cn and hold in back, k2, k3 from cn

sl 2 sts onto cn and hold in front, k3, k2 from cn

leg

NEXT RND: For front of leg: work Rnd 27 of Cable chart over 20 sts, place marker (pm), M1 for Rnd 1 of Flower chart; for back of leg: work LRI in first st (counts as 1/1 LC at beg of chart) work next 16 sts in patt from Rnd 27 of Cable chart, work LRI in last back of leg st (counts as 1/1 RC at end of chart), pm, M1 for Rnd 1 of Flower chart—42 sts: 21 sts each for front and back of leg.

NEXT RND: *Work Rnd 28 of Cable chart over 20 sts, slip marker (sl m), work Rnd 2 of Flower chart, inc to 3 sts as shown on chart; rep from *—46 sts.

Cont in patts as established until Rnd 16 of Flower chart has been completed, inc in flower panels on Rnds 4 and 14 as shown on chart—54 sts total: 27 sts each for front and back of leg, 20 sts each cable panel, 7 sts each flower panel.

NOTE: *From here on, rep Rnds 17–32 of Flower chart for flower panels; do not rep Rnds 1–16 of Flower chart.*

Cont in established patts until a total of 112 leg rnds have been completed above the joining rnd or to desired length (see Notes), ending with Rnd 28 of Cable chart and Rnd 32 of Flower chart—leg measures about 18″ (45.5 cm) from joining rnd. Knit 2 rnds.

EYELET RND: *K2tog, yo; rep from *.

Knit 1 rnd.

Using Jeny's Surprisingly Stretchy method (see Glossary), BO all sts—leg measures about 18½″ (47 cm) from joining rnd.

finishing

Weave in loose ends. Wet-block (see Glossary) and let dry thoroughly, stretching top of stockings wider as desired.

LACE EDGING *(make 2)*

With CC and size 10 (6 mm) needles, use the cable or long-tail method (see Glossary) to loosely CO 81 sts. Change to size 8 (5 mm) needles. Purl 1 WS row. Work Rows 1–16 of Lace chart. With size 10 (6 mm) needles, loosely BO all sts. Cut yarn, leaving a 24″ (61 cm) tail.

Block lightly by misting with water to about 19″ (48.5 cm) wide and 4″ (10 cm) high, pinning out points along the CO edge. Let air-dry thoroughly.

Turn stocking inside out. Hold lace edging and stocking tog with RS of lace facing WS of stocking so RS of lace will show when edging is folded to the outside. Beg and ending in the center of the back cable panel, pin lace around the top of the stocking with the BO edge of the lace piece about ¼″ (6 mm) down from BO edge of stocking, easing to fit. Sew lace edging to stocking as invisibly as possible using CC threaded on a tapestry needle; avoid sewing too close to eyelet holes.

Turn stockings right side out. Thread ribbon through eyelet rnd, beg and ending in center of back cable panel. Fold lace edging down over top of stocking as shown, and tie ribbon in a bow or knot, as desired.

FINISHED SIZE

About 6¼" (16 cm) circumference at top of hand, unstretched; will stretch to fit up to 7¼" (18.5 cm) circumference. See Notes for adjusting size.

YARN

Sportweight (#2 Fine).

SHOWN HERE: Quince & Co. Sparrow (100% linen; 168 yd [154 m]/50 g): natural, 1 skein.

NEEDLES

CUFF: size U.S. 2 (2.75 mm): straight or 24" (60 cm) circular (cir) needle.

HAND: size U.S. 1 (2.25 mm): set of 4 or 5 double-pointed (dpn) or two 24" (60 cm) cir needles or one 40" (100 cm) cir needle, depending on your chosen method for working in the round.

Adjust needle size if necessary to obtain the correct gauge.

NOTIONS

Markers (m); cable needle (cn); stitch holders; smooth cotton waste yarn for provisional cast-on; tapestry needle.

GAUGE

20 sts and 28 rows = 4" (10 cm) in garter st on larger needles.

36 sts and 36 rnds = 4" (10 cm) in lace patt from chart on smaller needles, unstretched.

noémie

LACE MITTS

Aside from the corsets and stays of pre-1920s wardrobes (not to mention the equally restrictive views on a woman's place in the world), I could easily have slipped into a silk dressing gown and a pair of fingerless gloves such as Noémie, and as a woman of leisure, traveled the continent via the Orient Express. At least for a while, until I think of how being waited upon hand and foot would have bored me to tears. But it is a great fantasy, *non*?

Perhaps because I labor with my hands in my many crafty endeavors, gloves have always fascinated me. I enjoy the metaphoric (and obviously virtual) protection they afford and, even in their daintiest versions, their service as a tiny buffer against the incivility of the world. For hundreds of years, whole guilds of glove makers (*gantiers*) held court in Paris, trading in everything from perfumed leather models (oh, to have a pair of those!) to knitted silks and wools. Apparently the latter variety required a rigorous apprenticeship where inferior work was seized and burned; I don't think I would have made the cut!

Noémie's lacy linen, short *gants* offer up an equal dose of Prairie Girl and Victoriana, and would have been equally fashionable at a Highgate garden party or for slinking around a depression-era New Orleans speakeasy. Don't let the tiny needles or fear of hard-to-knit fiber put you off—Sparrow from Quince & Co. is the most delicious linen yarn I've ever used.

notes

The garter-stitch cuffs are worked back and forth in rows with picots along the selvedge that form the lower edge of the mitt. After joining the beginning and end of each cuff, stitches are picked up along the plain selvedge edge and worked in the round to the top of the hand.

Working with linen yarn can be challenging because it is slippery and splits easily. You may find that bamboo or wooden needles work better for this project than metal needles.

Because it has very little memory, linen can stretch a lot during blocking. Work a generous swatch and wet-block it before beginning to ensure proper fit; adjust the needle sizes if necessary.

To make larger or smaller mitts, go up or down a needle size for the hand and fine-tune the fit by blocking.

cuff (make 2)

With larger needles and using a provisional method (see Glossary), CO 15 sts.

ROW 1: (RS) Knit.

ROW 2: (WS) Use the cable method (see Glossary) to CO 2 sts, then BO 2 sts to form picot, knit to end—no change to st count.

Rep these 2 rows 38 more times, ending with Row 2—78 rows and 39 garter ridges completed; piece measures about 11" (28 cm) from CO.

Cut yarn, leaving a 24" (61 cm) tail for grafting.

Carefully remove waste yarn from provisional CO and place the 15 exposed sts on an empty needle. Thread tail on tapestry needle use the Kitchener st for garter st (see Glossary) to graft live sts tog with sts from base of provisional CO.

HAND

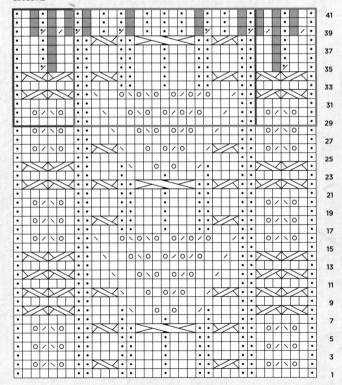

41
39
37
35
33
31
29
27
25
23
21
19
17
15
13
11
9
7
5
3
1

	knit
·	purl
o	yo
/	k2tog
\	ssk
⁄	p2tog
▨	no stitch
	sts for right back and left palm
	sts for right palm and left back

sl 1 st onto cn and hold in front, k2, k1 from cn

sl 2 sts onto cn and hold in back k1, k2 from cn

sl 3 sts onto cn and hold in front, k3, p1, k3 from cn

right mitt

HAND

Lay cuff flat with picot edge at the bottom, plain selvedge running across the top, and with grafted join in the center of the side facing you. Count out 10 garter ridges to the right of the graft along the top of the cuff and join yarn at this position. With smaller dpn and RS facing, pick up and knit 70 sts evenly spaced around entire top edge of cuff (about 9 sts for every 5 garter ridges or 10 rows), place marker (pm), and join for working in rnds. Rnd begins at little finger at the start of the back-of-hand sts; the grafted join is centered on the back of the hand.

NEXT RND: Work Rnd 1 of Hand chart over 35 sts for back-of-hand, pm at thumb side of mitt, then work Rnd 1 of chart again over 35 sts for palm.

Work even in patt until Rnd 28 of chart has been completed—piece measures 3¼" (8.5) from pick-up rnd.

NEXT RND: (Rnd 29 of chart) Work Sts 1–28 (outlined in green) for back of hand, place next 14 sts on holder for thumb removing m in center when you come to it, place new m for side of hand, work Sts 8–35 (outlined in purple) for palm—56 sts rem.

Cont in established patt until Rnd 41 has been completed, dec as shown on chart—42 sts rem; 21 sts each for palm and back of hand; piece measures 4½" (11.5 cm) from pick-up rnd.

NOTE: *There will be 2 purl sts next to each other at the boundaries between the back and palm.*

Loosely BO all sts as they appear (knit the knits and purl the purls).

THUMB

Return 14 held thumb sts onto needles and join yarn with RS facing. Pick up and knit 1 st from base of upper hand sts at thumb gap, k14 thumb sts, pick up and knit 1 st from base of upper hand sts, pm, and join for working in rnds—16 sts total.

Knit 2 rnds or until thumb measures ¼" (6 mm) less than desired length. Work in k1, p1 rib for 2 rnds.

Loosely BO all sts in established rib patt.

left mitt

HAND

Lay rem cuff flat with picot edge at the bottom, plain selvedge running across the top, and with grafted join in the center of the side facing you. Count out 10 garter ridges to the left of the graft along the top of the cuff and join yarn at this position. With smaller dpn and RS facing, pick up and knit 70 sts evenly spaced around entire top edge of cuff (about 9 sts for every 5 garter ridges or 10 rows), pm, and join for working in rnds. Rnd begins at little finger at the start of the palm sts; the grafted join is centered on the back of the hand.

NEXT RND: Work Rnd 1 of Hand chart over 35 sts for palm, pm at thumb side of mitt, then work Rnd 1 of chart over 35 sts for back of hand.

Work even in patt until Rnd 28 of chart has been completed—piece measures 3¼" (8.5) from pick-up rnd.

NEXT RND: (Rnd 29 of chart) Work Sts 1–28 (outlined in green) for palm, place next 14 sts on holder for thumb removing m in center when you come to it, place new m for side of hand, work Sts 8–35 (outlined in purple) for back of hand—56 sts rem.

Cont in established patt until Rnd 41 has been completed, dec as shown on chart—42 sts rem; 21 sts each for palm and back of hand; piece measures 4½" (11.5 cm) from pick-up rnd. As for right mitt, there will be 2 purl sts next to each other at the boundaries between the back of hand and palm.

Loosely BO all sts as they appear.

Work thumb as for right mitt.

finishing

RUCHED CUFF

Thread an 8" (20.5 cm) length of yarn on a tapestry needle and anchor it on the WS of the cuff close to the picot edge of the grafted join. Working upward from the picot edge to the hand pick-up rnd, sew a line of small running stitches (see Glossary) along the grafted join. Pull the end of the sewing yarn to gather the grafting line of the cuff to about 1" (2.5 cm) long. Sew gathers securely on WS, then fasten off end of gathering yarn securely.

Weave in loose ends. Block as desired.

FINISHED SIZE

About 7½" (19 cm) foot circumference and 9" (23 cm) long from back of heel to tip of toe, unstretched. Foot length is adjustable.

Will stretch to about 10" (25.5 cm) foot length, which fits a woman's size U.S. 9 shoe.

YARN

Fingering weight (#1 Super Fine).

SHOWN HERE: Shibui Knits Staccato (65% superwash merino, 30% silk, 5% nylon; 191 yd [175 m]/ 50 g): #ST107 watermelon, 1 skein (see Notes).

NEEDLES

Size U.S. 2 (2.5 mm): two 24" (60 cm) circular (cir) or one 40" (100 cm) circular (cir) for magic-loop method.

Adjust needle size if necessary to obtain the correct gauge.

NOTIONS

Markers (m); removable markers; waste yarn for stitch holders; size G/6 (4.25 mm) crochet hook for picking up sts (optional); tapestry needle; 56" (142 cm) of ⅜" (1 cm) wide velvet ribbon; two ½" (1.3 cm) ball buttons.

GAUGE

15 sts and 20 rows/rnds = 2" (5 cm) in St st.

tutu

SLIPPERS

One sunny afternoon, after popping into a shoe-box–sized bakery near my house for an Americanized rendition of *chassons aux pommes* (literally "apple slippers"—flaky layers of *choux* pastry with ribbons of syrupy apple slices tucked inside), I went into deep longing for the real thing. You see, nothing can replace a French pastry made in France and eaten in France— that's what is so lovely about the fleeting pleasure of enjoying the experience.

And pine I did for real ballet slippers (and the classes that would accompany them) when I was six years old. I learned a hard, but useful, life lesson when I truly realized we were poor, and I could not have the coveted pink beribboned beauties. I was crushed, but undaunted. I cajoled my mother into teaching me the rudiments, and I think my father even constructed a coarse *barre* in a closet in our cabin. My love of dance has continued to this day, and it is as essential to my life as air and water.

Tutu was originally intended to be a *chasson*, which is more a foot enclosing, grandpa-like slipper (or *pantoufle*), but I bowed to that demonic designer's question, "what if . . .?" and before I knew it, there emerged ballet slippers in a fanciful color, complete with vintage velvet ribbon bow and buttons.

notes

A pair of slippers in the size shown used almost the entire skein of yarn. You may wish to purchase an extra skein if making larger slippers.

Tutu is worked from the toe-up, which makes sizing a breeze because you can try on the slipper as it is worked and turn the heel at just the right point for a perfect fit.

Use waste yarn for stitch holders to make it easier to try on the slipper in progress.

slipper

Using the invisible method and substituting a second cir needle for the waste yarn (see sidebar on page 23), CO 12 sts.

TOE

SET-UP RND: K12, place marker (pm), then use a separate needle to knit across 12 sts from base of provisional CO, pm—24 sts total; 12 sts each for instep and sole.

NOTE: *If your sts are arranged as 12 sts each on separate cir needles or 12 sts each on the two halves of a long cir needle, you can omit the markers and use the needle divisions to indicate the marker positions.*

RND 1: (inc rnd) *K1, work a left-slant lifted increase (LLI; see Glossary) from st on right needle tip, knit to marker (m), work LLI from st on right needle tip, slip marker (sl m); rep from * once more—4 sts inc'd; 2 sts inc'd each for sole and instep.

RND 2: Knit.

Rep Rnds 1 and 2 six more times, then work Rnd 1 once more—56 sts total; 28 sts each for instep and sole.

Work even in St st for 14 rnds—30 rnds total; piece measures about 3" (7.5 cm) from CO.

FOOT

NOTE: *Sts in the center of the instep are placed on a holder and the sole and instep sts on each side of the held sts are worked back and forth in rows for the foot.*

ROW 1: (RS) K28 for sole, knit the first 10 instep sts, place the next 8 instep sts for center top of foot on waste yarn holder, turn work, leaving rem instep sts unworked—48 sts rem; 28 sole sts; 10 instep sts each side of held sts.

ROW 2: (WS) P2tog, purl to end—1 st dec'd.

ROW 3: Ssk, knit to end—1 st dec'd.

Rep Rows 2 and 3 three more times, ending with a RS row—40 sts rem; 28 sole sts; 6 sts each side of instep. Work 32 rows even, ending with a RS row—piece measures 7" (18 cm) from CO; foot measures about 4" (10 cm) from where sts were placed on holder.

NOTE: *To adjust foot length, work more or fewer rows here until piece measures 2" (5 cm) less than desired total foot length; every 2 rows added or removed will lengthen or shorten the foot by a little less than ¼" (6 mm).*

GUSSET INCREASES

SET-UP ROW: (WS) P6, pm if you have not already done so, p28 sole sts, pm if necessary, p6—28 sole sts between markers for heel.

ROW 1: (RS) K6, sl m, k1, LLI from st on right needle tip, knit to m, work LLI from st on right needle tip, sl m, k6—2 sts inc'd; 1 st each side of marked heel sts.

ROW 2: (WS) Purl.

Rep Rows 1 and 2 five more times—52 sts total; 40 heel sts between m; 6 sts each side of marked heel sts; piece measures about 8¼" (21 cm) from CO.

HEEL TURN

Turn the heel using short-rows as foll:

ROW 1: (RS) K6, sl m, k23, ssk, k1, turn work.

ROW 2: (WS) Sl 1 purlwise with yarn in front (pwise wyf), p7, p2tog, p1, turn work.

ROW 3: Sl 1 pwise with yarn in back (wyb), knit to 1 st before turning gap, ssk (1 st on each side of gap), k1, turn work.

ROW 4: Sl 1 pwise wyf, purl to 1 st before turning gap, p2tog (1 st from each side of gap), p1, turn work.

Rep the last 2 rows 6 more times—36 sts rem; 24 heel sts between m; 6 sts each side of heel sts.

NEXT ROW: (RS) Sl pwise wyb, knit to 1 st before m, sl next st temporarily to right needle tip, remove m, return slipped st to left needle, ssk (last heel st tog with instep st after it), knit to end—35 sts rem.

NEXT ROW: (WS) Sl 1 pwise wyf, purl to 1 st before m, sl next st temporarily to right needle tip, remove m, return slipped st to left needle, p2tog (last heel st tog with instep st after it), purl to end—34 sts rem.

Place sts on holder.

Make a second slipper the same as the first.

finishing

INSTEP STRAPS AND LACE EDGING

With RS of sole facing, measure about 1" (2.5 cm) from held heel sts along each selvedge and place a removable marker. Work left and right slippers separately as foll:

Left slipper

Hold slipper with RS facing so that heel sts are at the bottom and toe sts are at the top. Rejoin yarn at removable marker position on right selvedge. Using optional crochet hook if desired, pick up and knit 8 sts along selvedge between m and held heel sts. Place picked-up sts on needle and work St st back and forth in rows for 29 rows, beg and ending with a WS row—strap measures about 3" (7.5 cm) from pick-up row. Try on slipper, draw strap across the front of the foot and see if it reaches to the marked 1" (2.5 cm) selvedge section on the other side of the slipper. Add or remove rows as necessary to achieve the proper strap length.

Dec to shape tip of strap as foll:

ROW 1: (RS) [Ssk] 2 times, [k2tog] 2 times—4 sts rem.

ROW 2: (WS) P2tog, ssp (see Glossary)—2 sts rem.

ROW 3: K2tog—1 st rem.

NEXT RND: With RS of strap facing and 1 rem strap st on right needle tip, use attached working yarn to pick up and knit 24 sts along left selvedge of strap, k34 held heel sts, pick up and knit 42 sts (about 1 st for every row) along one side of foot opening, k8 held sts in center of instep, pick up and knit 42 sts along other side of foot opening, and 24 sts along other selvedge of strap to end at tip—175 sts total.

EYELET RND: With RS still facing, use the decrease method (see Glossary) to BO 25 strap sts (1 st rem on right needle after last BO), then with RS still facing, transfer rem st on right needle tip to left needle, [yo, k2tog] 17 times across 34 heel sts, [yo, k2tog] 46 times around foot opening to end at base of strap, BO rem 24 strap sts—126 sts rem.

Cut yarn and fasten off last st.

With WS facing, rejoin yarn at base of strap ready to work across sts of foot opening and use the picot method to BO as foll: *Use the cable method (see Glossary) to CO 2 sts, BO 4 sts, return st from right needle tip to left needle; rep from * until 1 st rem, then fasten off last st.

Right slipper

Hold slipper with RS facing so that heel sts are at the bottom and toe sts are at the top. Rejoin yarn at removable marker position on left selvedge. Using optional crochet hook if desired, pick up and knit 8 sts along selvedge between held heel sts and removable m. Work strap as for left slipper—1 st rem at tip of strap.

NEXT RND: With RS of strap facing and 1 rem strap st on right needle tip, use attached working yarn to pick up and knit 24 sts along left selvedge of strap and 42 sts along one side of foot opening, k8 held sts in center of instep, pick up and knit 42 sts along other side of foot opening, k34 held heel sts, then pick up and knit 24 sts along other selvedge of strap to end at tip—175 sts total.

EYELET RND: With RS still facing, use the decrease method to BO 25 strap sts (1 st rem on right needle after last BO), then with RS still facing, transfer rem st from right needle to left needle, [yo, k2tog] 46 times around foot opening, [yo, k2tog] 17 times across heel sts, BO rem 24 strap sts—126 sts rem.

Cut yarn and fasten off last st at tip.

With WS facing, rejoin yarn at base of strap, ready to work across heel sts and use the picot method to BO as foll: *Use the cable method to CO 2 sts, BO 4 sts, return st from right needle to left needle; rep from * until 1 st rem, then fasten off last st.

Weave in loose ends. Wet-block, stretching to fit if necessary and pinning straps to lie flat.

BUTTON CLOSURE

Stretch strap across instep as shown and attach button centered on the strap tip about ½" (1.3 cm) from the end, sewing through both layers of the strap and the slipper.

RIBBON TIE

Cut two pieces of ribbon, each about 28" (71 cm) long. Beg and ending at center front instep, thread ribbon in and out of eyelet round, skipping the ribbon across the base of the strap on the inside of the slipper. Try on for correct fit, tie the ribbon in a bow, and trim both ends of ribbon on the diagonal.

FINISHED SIZE

About 7¼" (18.5 cm) foot circumference, unstretched (will stretch to
about 8" [20.5 cm] circumference),
and 10" (25.5 cm) long from back of
heel to tip of toe (will become shorter
when sock is stretched widthwise).

To fit women's U.S. shoe sizes 7½ to 8.

YARN

Fingering weight (#1 Super Fine).

SHOWN HERE: Quince & Co. Tern
(75% American wool, 25% silk; 221 yd
[202 m]/50 g); #142 oyster, 2 skeins
(see Notes).

NEEDLES

Size U.S. 2 (2.5 mm): two 24" (60 cm)
circular (cir) or one 40" (100 cm) cir
if using magic-loop method.

*Adjust needle size if necessary to obtain
the correct gauge.*

NOTIONS

Markers (m); stitch holder (optional);
tapestry needle.

GAUGE

15 sts and 23 rnds = 2" (5 cm) in St st,
worked in rnds.

20–23 sts of Plume chart panel
measure 3" (7.5 cm) wide, worked in
either rows or rnds.

32 rnds (2 vertical patt reps) of Plume
chart measure 3" (7.5 cm) high,
worked in rnds.

plume
ANKLETS

The sock knitters among you may have to cover your ears for
just a second—I had no desire to knit a single sock until I began writing this
book. I know, such heresy . . . how could I not want to use those adorably
tiny needles and divine hand-dyed yarns, not to mention experience the
satisfaction of making, and then wearing, my very own *chaussettes*. I never
understood the appeal until I began researching the subject. My goodness,
such a wealth of knitting information and so many decisions to make: the
myriad cast-ons, the heel choices, toe up or top down . . . where does one
begin? Couple this with the portability angle and I finally get it—win-win!

These flirty, lacy anklets worked from the toe up are designed to be as
light and soft as their French namesake, floating like the lovely plumage of
a young swan over the foot. Though the juvenile bird will eventually become
glossy black or white, it is a downy gray in the transition to adulthood; that
is where I am in my sock knitting . . . still a teenager. I have discovered that
I enjoy the toe-up method because I can knit socks that easily match my
narrow foot and never have the pesky problem of running out of yarn. The
heel I have been enchanted with lately is one that gives a very smooth look;
perfectly suited to me because of the retro sling backs I favor—the ideal
shoe for showing off the coy lace heel that I devised for Plume.

notes

Sock knitters all have their favorite methods of beginning toe-up socks. Personally, I prefer to use an invisible method that employs two circular needles (or one long circular), one of which substitutes for waste yarn (see sidebar on page 23).

Only a small amount of the second skein was needed for the socks shown.

The stitch count of the Plume chart varies from 20 to 23 sts. Always count the charted lace panel as 23 stitches, even if it happens to be on a round where it has temporarily decreased to fewer stitches.

If you adjust the foot length, make a note of the last instep chart row completed before starting the heel turn so you can begin the heel pattern with the correct row. For the lace version of the heel, the last 9 rows of the heel turn are worked with lace patterning on the center heel stitches. These 9 rows have to finish with the same chart row as worked over the instep stitches in the heel turn set-up row. If you work more or fewer rounds in the foot, you will need to count backward 9 rows from where your instep pattern ended to determine which chart row is your new first heel pattern row. For example, the socks shown here end the instep with Row 10 of the chart before turning the heel. Rows 11–19 of the Plume Heel chart correspond to Rows 2–10 of the Plume chart, so the heel ends with the equivalent of Row 10 of the main Plume pattern.

toe

Using the invisible method and substituting a second cir needle for the waste yarn (see sidebar on page 23), CO 12 sts.

SET-UP RND: K12, place marker (pm), then use a separate needle to knit across 12 sts from base of provisional CO, pm—24 sts total; 12 sts each for sole and instep.

NOTE: *If your sts are arranged as 12 sts each on separate cir needles or 12 sts each on the two halves of a long cir needle, you can omit the markers and use the needle divisions to indicate the marker positions.*

Rnd begins at start of instep sts. Inc for toe as foll:

RND 1: (inc rnd) *K1, work a right-slant lifted increase from base of next st on left needle tip, then knit the st itself (LRI; see Glossary), knit to last st before m, work LRI to inc 1 in last st, slip marker (sl m); rep from *—4 sts inc'd; 2 sts each for instep and sole.

RND 2: Knit.

Rep Rnds 1 and 2 six more times, then work Rnd 1 once more—56 sts total; 28 sts each for instep and sole.

NEXT 4 RNDS: Knit.

NEXT RND: *Knit to 2 sts before m, k2tog, sl m; rep from *—2 sts dec'd; 54 sts rem; 27 sts each for instep and sole—piece measures 1¾" (4.5 cm) from CO.

foot

SET-UP RND: K2, work Rnd 1 of Plume chart over center 23 instep sts, k2, sl m, k27 sole sts.

Working sts outside the chart panel in St st, work Rnds 2–16 of Plume chart once, work Rnds 1–16 two times, then work Rnds 1–5 once again—53 chart rnds completed; piece measures 6½" (16.5 cm) from CO. To adjust foot length, cont in patt until foot measures 3½" (9 cm) less than desired length from tip of toe to back of heel before starting gusset incs (see Notes).

increase for gusset

RND 1: (inc rnd) K2, work chart patt as established to last 2 instep sts, k2, sl m, k1, work LRI to inc 1 in next st, knit to last st, work LRI to inc 1 in last st—2 sts inc'd on sole.

RND 2: Work even in established patt.

Rep the last 2 rnds 9 more times, ending with Rnd 9 of chart—74 sts total; 27 instep sts; 47 sole sts; piece measures 8¼" (21 cm) from CO.

TURN HEEL

SET-UP RND: K2, work Rnd 10 of chart to last 2 instep sts, k2, then place sts just worked on optional holder or allow them to rest on a separate cir needle while working the heel—27 instep sts on holder; 47 sole sts rem.

Work 47 sole sts back and forth in short-rows as foll:

ROW 1: (RS) K26, ssk, k1, turn work.

ROW 2: (WS) Sl 1 as if to purl with yarn in front (pwise wyf), p6, p2tog, p1, turn work.

ROW 3: Sl 1 pwise with yarn in back (wyb), knit to 1 st before gap formed on previous RS row, ssk (1 st each side of gap), k1, turn work.

ROW 4: Sl 1 pwise wyf, purl to 1 st before gap formed on previous WS row, p2tog (1 st each side of gap), turn work.

ROWS 5–10: Rep Rows 3 and 4 three more times, ending with a WS row—37 heel sts rem.

Cont according to your choice of heel as foll:

PLUME HEEL

PLUME

☐	knit on RS rows and all rnds; purl on WS rows
•	purl on RS rows and all rnds; knit on WS rows
O	yo
╱	k2tog on RS rows and all rnds; p2tog on WS rows
╲	ssk on RS rows and all rnds; ssp on WS rows
V	sl 1 pwise wyb on RS rows; sl 1 pwise wyf on WS rows
⅄	k3tog
人	sssk (see Glossary)
▨	no stitch
▨	unworked sts each side during heel shaping

Cont as foll:

ROWS 11–19: Work in patt from Plume Heel chart—28 heel sts rem; 26 sts between turning gaps and 2 sts at beg of row before first turning gap.

Return 27 held instep sts to needle. Resume working in patt from Plume chart as foll:

RND 20: (joining rnd) Using yarn attached to end of last RS heel row, work across instep sts as: k2, work Rnd 11 of Plume chart to last 2 instep sts, k2; work first unworked heel st as k1, work second unworked heel st tog with st after it as: k2tog, work entire Rnd 11 of chart over 23 sts, k1, sl last heel st to beg of instep needle—piece measures 10" (25.5 cm) from CO.

NEXT RND: Work slipped heel st tog with first instep st as: k2tog, k1, work Rnd 12 of chart to last 2 instep sts, k1, work last instep st tog with first heel st after it as: ssk, pm, k1, work Rnd 12 of chart to last heel st, k1—2 sts at each side of marked patt on front of leg; 1 st at each side of marked patt on back of leg.

Rnd begins at start of front-of-leg sts.

leg

NEXT RND: K2, work Rnd 13 of chart to last 2 front-of-leg sts, k2, sl m, k1, work Rnd 13 of chart to last back-of-leg st, k1.

Keeping sts outside chart panels in St st, work Rnds 14–16 of chart once, then work Rnds 1–16 two more times—leg measures about 3½" (9 cm) from joining rnd; 7 complete 16-rnd chart reps completed from start of foot. For a longer leg, cont in patt until leg measures ½" (1.3 cm) less than desired total length.

hemmed cuff

Knit 2 rnds.

PICOT FOLD RND: *K2tog, yo; rep from *.

Knit 3 rnds.

Using the sewn method (see Glossary), BO all sts. Cut yarn, leaving 24" (61 cm) tail. Fold cuff in half along picot fold rnd and sew hem in place, working loosely enough so the cuff can stretch over the heel.

finishing

Weave in loose ends. Wet-block (see Glossary), stretching gently to open up lace pattern.

Plain stockinette heel

ROWS 11–20: Rep Rows 3 and 4 five more times, ending with a WS row—27 heel sts rem; all heel sts have been worked—piece measures 10" (25.5 cm) from CO.

Return 27 held instep sts to needle.

JOINING RND: Sl 1 pwise wyb, k25 heel sts, sl last heel st to beg of instep sts, pm, work last heel st tog with first instep st as k2tog, k1, work Rnd 11 of chart to last 2 instep sts, k1, work last instep st tog with slipped first heel st as ssk, pm, k1, work Rnd 11 of chart to last heel st, k1—52 sts; 27 instep sts for front of leg, 25 heel sts for back of leg.

Rnd begins at start of front-of-leg sts.

NEXT RND: K2, work Rnd 12 of chart to last 2 front-of-leg sts, k2, sl m, k1, work Rnd 12 of chart to last back-of-leg st, k1.

Skip to Leg instructions.

Lace patterned heel

NOTE: *When working the Plume Heel chart patt back and forth in rows, odd-numbered chart rows are RS rows, and even-numbered chart rows are WS rows. After completing Row 10 of the heel turning instructions above and before introducing the lace patt, the 37 heel sts will be arranged as 17 sts between the turning gaps and 10 unworked sts at each side.*

FINISHED SIZE

About 7½" (19 cm) hand circumference, including 1" (2.5 cm) overlapped edgings, and 8½" (21.5 cm) long overall.

YARN

DK and worsted weights (#3 Light and #4 Medium).

SHOWN HERE: Rowan Kid Classic (70% wool, 26% mohair, 4% nylon; 153 yd [140 m]/ 50 g): #832 peat (black; MC), 1 ball.

Louisa Harding Grace (50% merino; 50% silk; 110 yd [101 m]/50 g): #01 white (CC), 1 ball.

NEEDLES

Size U.S. 5 (3.75 mm): one 24" (60 cm) circular (cir) and set of 4 or 5 double-pointed (dpn).

Adjust needle size if necessary to obtain the correct gauge.

NOTIONS

Markers (m); removable markers; stitch holders; tapestry needle, ten ⅝" (1.6 cm) buttons; 18" (45.5 cm) of ½" or ¾" (1.3 or 2 cm) wide grosgrain ribbon in color to match MC (optional); sharp-point sewing needle and matching thread.

GAUGE

21½ sts and 36 rows = 4" (10 cm) in French weave patt.

gabrielle
BUTTONED MITTS

These oh-so-very Chanel-like graphic black-and-white side-buttoned *mittaines* bring together everything I adore about design: an easy-to-create project with unexpected details that elevate the style quotient. Fans of Madame Coco will appreciate the confident, yet elegant aesthetic that allows Gabrielle to be worn with anything from leather to velvet.

As a designer, Chanel possessed a chameleon-like ability to recalibrate and innovate, yet stay true to her core vision. I find it interesting that she was raised in very rough country, far from that glamorous world she later created for herself. Having traveled through the regions where she spent her youth, I can assure you, central France is not for sissies—it is endowed with a wild volcanic landscape that demands self-reliance and resourcefulness. Knowing this deepens my understanding of what fostered Coco's self-assurance and increases my admiration of her accomplishments in a time when women were practically invisible within the cosmos of *haute couture*.

Oh, to have been a (well-dressed) fly on the wall of her Rue Chambon 1920s *atelier* as she deliberated on the first of her many groundbreaking undertakings—the dress that brought black out of mourning and into the light of day. Many of the early sewing projects that I labored over were Vogue patterns from the Parisian *couturiers*—Lanvin, Dior, Givenchy. I was their willing apprentice and, because of them, I have the good fortune to make designing my work today. *Coco, je t'aime!*

notes

Choose your yarns carefully if making substitutions. I intended to work the entire project using the same yarn for both colors. The cream-colored DK weight Kid Classic was missing the "pop" I wanted for the white portion of the design. A swatch worked entirely in worsted-weight Grace was too soft for a hardworking mitt—if there can ever be such a thing. Using both yarns made for the perfect marriage.

Both mitts are worked the same. Right- and left-handedness is determined by the placement of the buttons during finishing.

stitch guide

French Weave (multiple of 4 sts + 3)
NOTE: *Slip all sts as if to purl (pwise).*

ROW 1: (RS) With CC, k1, sl 1 with yarn in front (wyf), k1, *sl 1 with yarn in back (wyb), k1, sl 1 wyf, k1; rep from *.

ROW 2: (WS) With CC, p3, *sl 1 wyf, p3; rep from *.

ROW 3: With MC, k1, *sl 1 wyb, k3; rep from * to last 2 sts, sl 1 wyb, k1.

ROW 4: With MC, purl.

ROW 5: With CC, k1, sl 1 wyb, k1, *sl 1 wyf, k1, sl 1 wyb, k1; rep from *.

ROW 6: With CC, p1, *sl 1 wyf, p3; rep from * to last 2 sts, sl 1 wyf, p1.

ROW 7: With MC, k3, *sl 1 wyb, k3; rep from *.

ROW 8: With MC, purl.

Rep Rows 1–8 for patt.

Seed Stitch (odd number of sts)
ALL ROWS: K1, *p1, k1; rep from *.

Seed Stitch (even number of sts)
ROW 1: (WS) *K1, p1; rep from *.

ROW 2: (RS) *P1, k1; rep from *.

Rep Rows 1 and 2 for patt.

left mitt

CUFF

With MC and cir needle, use the cable method (see Glossary) to CO 35 sts. Work back and forth in rows as foll:

ROW 1: (RS) With MC, p1, *k1, p1; rep from *.

ROW 2: (WS) With MC, k1, *p1, k1; rep from *.

ROWS 3 and 4: With CC, k1, *slip 1 as if to purl with yarn in back (pwise wyb), k1; rep from *.

ROWS 5 and 6: With MC, knit.

ROWS 7–21: Rep Rows 3–6 three times (do not rep Rows 1 and 2), then work Rows 3–5 once more.

ROW 22: (WS) With MC, purl—piece measures 2" (5 cm) from CO.

HAND

Work Rows 1–7 of French weave patt (see Stitch Guide).

NEXT ROW: (WS; Row 8 of patt) With MC, p17, place marker (pm), purl into front and back of next st (p1f&b), pm, p17—36 sts; 2 thumb gusset sts between m.

NOTE: *When increasing for the thumb gusset, maintain the established pattern for the stitches on each side of the gusset so the pattern will flow properly across these stitches when they are rejoined above the thumb; work the gusset stitches into the pattern as well as possible.*

Work Rows 1–5 of patt once more.

INC ROW: (WS; Row 6 of patt) Work in patt to m, slip marker (sl m), M1P (see Glossary) in color required by patt, work in patt to next m, M1P in color required by patt, sl m, work in patt to end—2 sts inc'd inside gusset m.

Working new sts into patt, [work 5 rows even, then rep the inc row] 3 times—10 gusset sts between m; 44 sts total. Work Rows 1–4 of patt once more—36 patt rows completed; piece measures 6″ (15 cm) from CO.

NEXT ROW: (RS; Row 5 of patt) Work in patt to first gusset m, remove m and place 10 gusset sts on holder, remove second gusset m, use the backward-loop method (see Glossary) to CO 1 st over thumb gap, work in patt to end—35 sts.

Resume working established patt across all sts and work Rows 6–8 of patt once, Rows 1–8 once, then Rows 1–4 once more, ending with a WS row—52 patt rows completed; piece measures 7¾″ (19.5 cm) from CO. With MC, work in seed st (see Stitch Guide) for 4 rows, ending with a WS row. BO in patt on next RS row until 1 st rem, but do not break yarn—piece measures 8½″ (21.5 cm) from CO.

SIDE EDGINGS

With RS facing and using yarn attached at end of BO, pick up and knit 49 more sts along selvedge of top edging, French weave patt, and cuff to CO edge—50 sts total. Work in seed st for 6 rows, ending with a RS row. With WS facing, BO all sts in patt—edging measures about 1″ (2.5 cm) from pick-up row. With RS facing, join MC to CO edge of rem selvedge, pick up and knit 50 sts along entire edge. Work in seed st for 6 rows, ending with a RS row. With WS facing, BO all sts in patt—second side edging measures about 1″ (2.5 cm) from pick-up row.

THUMB

Place 10 held thumb sts on dpn. With RS facing, join MC to beg of thumb sts.

NEXT RND: Knit across thumb sts inc 2 sts evenly spaced, then pick up and knit 2 sts from base of st CO over thumb gap—14 sts total.

Distribute sts as evenly as possible on 3 or 4 dpn, pm, and join for working in rnds.

RNDS 1 and 3: *K1, p1; rep from *.

RNDS 2 and 4: *P1, k1; rep from *.

BO all sts in seed st patt—thumb measures about ¾" (2 cm).

right mitt

Work as for left mitt (see Notes).

finishing

Wet-block (see Glossary), gently stretching to size if necessary. Weave in loose ends.

LEFT MITT

Hold mitt with RS facing and cuff at the bottom so that the back-of-hand is to the left of the thumb (end of RS rows) and the palm is to the right of the thumb (beg of RS rows). Using removable markers, mark placement of five buttons centered on the RS of the back-of-hand side edging, the first ½" (1.3 cm) up from the CO edge, the second 1" (2.5 cm) down from the BO edge, and the rem three evenly spaced in between. If using the optional reinforcing ribbon, cut a length of ribbon slightly shorter than the length of the side edgings. Overlap the back-of-hand edging on top of the palm edging with the ribbon sandwiched in between. With sewing needle and thread, sew buttons to marked positions, sewing through all layers. Turn mitt inside-out. With WS facing and MC threaded on a tapestry needle, invisibly sew the BO edge of palm-side edging to the pick-up row at the base of the back-of-hand edging.

RIGHT MITT

Hold mitt with RS facing and cuff at the bottom so that the palm is to the left of the thumb (end of RS rows) and the back-of-hand is to the right of the thumb (beg of RS rows). Using removable markers, mark placement of five buttons centered on the top layer of the back-of-hand side edging, the first ½" (1.3 cm) up from the CO edge, the second 1" (2.5 cm) down from the BO edge, and the rem three evenly spaced in between. Complete as for left mitt.

Les étoles et les cache-coeurs

SHAWLS AND WRAPS

ALTHOUGH IN THE STRICTEST SENSE, A *CACHE-COEUR* SIGNIFIES A GARMENT THAT HIDES OR PROTECTS THE HEART, I am taking some liberties here (because I love the term) to use it to group together this collection of shrugs and shoulder coverings. Well-bred ladies of all stripes have always relied on a discreet stole or shrug for a bit of protection when a gown might be too scanty or the occasion calls for elegant warmth. Their return to the knitting universe is a welcome one.

The garment whose name was formerly synonymous with "bed jacket" has become a much-desired *accoutrement*. For my daughter's dear friend's nuptials, I could not resist creating an airy confection of silk and mohair to float delicately above her lovely wedding dress. What a delight to fashion moonlight-soft yarn into something as graceful as a bird's wing!

The essential element is adaptability—work with your own proportions until the silhouette is in balance. Choose your yarn and needles carefully to ensure appealing drape. The cushy, soft, faux-crochet Gitane (page 82) works with just such a delicious fiber.

Any figure type can wear a *cache-coeur*, but it takes a bit of tinkering and, in the case of those worked from the top down, the addition of short-rows or lengthening of the sleeves or body. The Alouette bolero (page 88) would be a snap to fashion into a longer garment if desired (see page 118 for books that will help you customize your garments).

Shawls in France are called *étoles* or *châles*—words that are unquestionably more romantic sounding than "wrap." Many a well-to-do lady's form was graced with a luxurious woven *châle* of pashmina and cashmere in mid nineteenth-century Europe. So, where are the knitted wraps and stoles from France? There is evidence of them in paintings and the written word, but little history remains. Northern Europe and Russian archives are replete with sterling examples of knitted shawls created by everyday folk, but much of the finely wrought needlework in France (both bobbin and knitted lace and finely embroidered garments) was in the skilled hands of nuns.

In the forthcoming chapter, the chic *étole* Tattoo (page 94) is as far from that chaste white handiwork as could be with its mysterious, twining twists of very modern fiber. The amber-hued Safran (page 98) gives one the opportunity to work in the simplest of stitches with an unconventional finishing technique that converts it in a flash from a shawl to a wrap. The Morgaine hood (page 102) is a changeling that can become either a secretive cloaked cowl or a draped shoulder covering in a few easy steps.

I invite you to wrap up in something *trés chic* next time you need to warm your heart!

About 40" (101.5 cm) circumference at bustline and 9¼" (23.5 cm) long from center back neck to lower edge.

YARN

Chunky (#5 Bulky).

SHOWN HERE: Blue Sky Alpacas Suri Merino (60% baby suri alpaca, 40% merino; 164 yd [150 m]/100 g): #410 snow, 2 skeins.

NEEDLES

BODY: size U.S. 15 (10 mm): 24" (60 cm) or longer circular (cir).

SLEEVES: size U.S. 10½ (6.5 mm): set of 4 or 5 double-pointed (dpn).

Adjust needle size if necessary to obtain the correct gauge.

NOTIONS

Marker (m); stitch holders; tapestry needle, 75" (190 cm) of ⅜" (1 cm) silk or grosgrain ribbon.

GAUGE

69 sts after dividing body and sleeves measure about 40" (101.5 cm) wide, and 12 yoke rows measure about 4" (10 cm) high in patt from shrug instructions.

Exact gauge is not critical for this project; aim for a very open, lacy appearance.

gitane

LACY SHRUG

My door to the world of needlework was opened not with a needle, but with a crochet hook. I am quite fond of being "bi-stitchual," as some who work in both disciplines call themselves. As a designer, crochet has given me a great back story from which to create sculptural, seamless (and lacy) garments. There is no reason a knitter could not become a crochet lover as well (and vice versa). If you are a visual-type knitter who adores charts, the wealth of diagrammed crochet patterns (check out the French and Japanese offerings) will have you rummaging through your knitting basket for that hook you thought you would use only for crab-stitch edgings.

During the vagabond years of my youth, I carried a small carpetbag of yarn and assorted hooks. I churned out rainbow-striped caps and scarves for any willing wearer and honed my craft with unappealingly scratchy yarns while leaving a crocheted trail across the miles at every hippie haven on the West Coast. When a more sedentary (and sane) life beckoned, I added knitting to my repertoire, but perennially searched for a way to make some of my designs more crochet-like. For Gitane, I chose angelic suri merino yarn from Blue Sky Alpacas, which encircles the shoulders like a floating cloud. The featherweight crochet-like stitch pattern is ideal for this airy garment, which would have been far too weighty in a more solid stitch. Use the ribbon ties to cinch up the front panel or let it fly free as a bird's wing.

notes

Gitane can be worn myriad ways. Experiment with how tightly or loosely to draw up the neckline ribbon for different effects. For larger bust sizes, distribute more gathers toward the front.

The suri alpaca/merino-blend yarn shown here is exquisitely soft, but also tends to shed a bit. Be aware of this when wearing the shrug with darker garments.

The pattern used in Gitane is an amalgam of my favorite crochet-look knitting stitches, which involve double yarnovers and purling 3, 4, or 5 stitches together. If you have never worked with larger needles when purling multiple stitches together, practice a bit with a swatch beforehand. See the sidebar on page 85 for tips on working these stitches with larger needles.

The neckline circumference shown on the schematic is without the ribbon drawstring. Adjust the ribbon to draw in the neck opening for the desired fit.

stitch guide

Work 2 sts in double yo: Knit into the front of the first double yo loop, then knit into the back of the second double yo loop—2 sts worked in double yo.

NOTE: *When checking stitch counts, each double yo counts as 2 sts.*

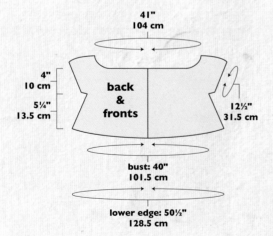

41"
104 cm

4"
10 cm

5¼"
13.5 cm

back & fronts

12½"
31.5 cm

bust: 40"
101.5 cm

lower edge: 50½"
128.5 cm

shrug

YOKE

With cir needle and using the cable method (see Glossary), CO 44 sts.

SET-UP ROW: (WS) K1, *yo twice, k1; rep from *—130 sts, counting each double yo as 2 sts.

ROW 1: (RS) K1, *work 2 sts in double yo (see Stitch Guide), k1; rep from *.

ROW 2: *K1, p3tog; rep from * to last 2 sts, k2tog—65 sts rem.

ROW 3: Knit.

ROW 4: K1, *yo twice, k1; rep from *—193 sts.

ROW 5: Rep Row 1.

ROW 6: *K1, p3tog; rep from * to last st, k1—97 sts.

ROW 7: Knit.

ROW 8: Rep Row 4—289 sts.

ROW 9: Rep Row 1.

ROW 10: *K1, p4tog; rep from * to last 4 sts, p4tog—115 sts rem.

ROW 11: (dividing row; RS) K17 for left front, temporarily sl next st to right needle, place next 22 sts on holder for left sleeve, return slipped st to left needle and work it tog with the first back st as k2tog, k33 back sts, temporarily sl next st to right needle, place next 22 sts on holder for right sleeve, return slipped st to left needle tip and work it tog with first st of right front as k2tog, k17 for right front—69 sts rem; 12 rows completed including set-up row; piece measures about 4" (10 cm) from CO.

LOWER BODY

ROW 12: (WS) K1, [yo twice, k1] 14 times, k3tog, k1, [yo twice, k1] 31 times, k3tog, k1, [yo twice, k1] 15 times—185 sts.

ROW 13: (RS) [K1, work 2 sts in double yo] 15 times, work the next (k1, k3tog, k1) of previous row tog as k3tog, [work 2 sts in double yo, k1] 30 times, work 2 sts in double yo, work the next (k1, k3tog, k1) of previous row tog as k3tog, [work 2 sts in double yo, k1] 14 times—181 sts rem.

ROW 14: *K1, p4tog; rep from * to last st, k1—73 sts rem.

ROW 15: Knit.

ROW 16: K1, *yo twice, k1; rep from *—217 sts.

ROW 17: K1, *work 2 sts in double yo, k1; rep from *.

ROW 18: *K1, p4tog; rep from * to last 2 sts, k2tog—87 sts rem.

ROWS 19–21: Rep Rows 15–17 once more—259 sts after Row 20.

ROW 22: *K1, p5tog; rep from * to last st, k1—87 sts rem.

ROWS 23–25: Rep Rows 15–17 once more—259 sts after Row 24.

ROW 26: *K1, p5tog; rep from * to last st, k1—87 sts rem.

NOTE: *For a longer body, rep Rows 23–26 as many times as desired; every 4-row rep added will lengthen the piece by about 1¼" (3.2 cm).*

ROW 27: Knit—lower body measures about 5¼" (13.5 cm) from dividing row.

Loosely BO all sts using the picot method as foll: K2, BO 1 st (1 st rem on right needle tip); *sl st on right needle tip to left needle tip, use the cable method to CO 1 st, BO 2 sts; rep from * until 1 st rem, then fasten off last st.

WORKING MULTIPLE STITCHES TOGETHER WITH LARGE NEEDLES

Working several stitches together can be challenging even with smaller needles. Add large needles to the mix and you might have a recipe for frustration. For ease of working, it is imperative that these stitches are not too tight on the needles; otherwise, it will be nearly impossible to insert a needle through all of them at the same time. Before you work the group of stitches together, use the right needle tip to gently tug the loops open while they are still on the left needle. Making sure that the yarn is in the back for a knit stitch or in the front for a purl stitch, insert the right needle well into all the stitches that need to be worked together. To complete the stitch, wrap the working yarn over the right needle tip and pull the loop through all of the stitches. If your yarn is slippery or thick, you may want to hold onto the bottom of the stitches to be worked together to keep them together and make sure none are missed. Keep in mind, practice makes perfect!

sleeves

Place 22 held sleeve sts onto 3 dpn. With RS facing, join yarn to end of held sts. Pick up and knit 5 sts across base of armhole, k22 sleeve sts, place marker (pm), and join for working in rnds—27 sts. Redistribute sts as evenly as possible on 3 or 4 dpn. Knit 4 rnds—sleeve measures about 1" (2.5 cm). To adjust sleeve length, work even in St st until sleeve measures desired length. Use Jeny's Surprisingly Stretchy Method (see Glossary), to BO all sts.

finishing

To avoid flattening the stitch pattern, this piece was not blocked. If blocking is desired, take care to make a large preliminary swatch and evaluate how blocking will affect the appearance and dimensions of the fabric.

Weave in loose ends.

Trim each end of ribbon on the diagonal. Thread ribbon on a tapestry needle, and beg and ending at center front, weave the ribbon through the double-yo holes of the yoke set-up row as shown. Pull the ends of the ribbon to gather the neckline and tie where best fit is achieved.

FINISHED SIZE

About 32 (36½, 40, 44½)" (81.5 [92.5, 101.5, 113] cm) bust circumference.

Shrug shown measures 32" (81.5 cm).

YARN

Chunky weight (#5 Bulky).

SHOWN HERE: Louisa Harding Millais (50% wool, 50% acrylic; 65 yd [59 m]/50 g): #11 sailor (dark blue), 4 (4, 5, 6) balls.

NEEDLES

BODY AND SLEEVES: size U.S. 10½ (6.5 mm): 24" (60 cm) circular (cir) and set of 4 or 5 double-pointed (dpn).

NECK EDGING: size U.S. 11 (8 mm): 24" (60 cm) cir.

Adjust needle size if necessary to obtain the correct gauge.

NOTIONS

Markers (m); stitch holders; tapestry needle; decorative shank button (optional); small piece of backing fabric to reinforce button (optional); size K/10½ (6.5 mm) crochet hook for button closure (optional).

GAUGE

14 sts and 18 rows = 4" (10 cm) in St st on smaller needles.

alouette

SHRUG

"Alouette, gentille alouette" . . . how many of us sang that song when we were young? I imagined the skylark in the lyrics to be a lovely bluebird blue. Imagine my surprise when it turned out to be a rather plain specimen (all the better for survival, I suppose)! Hopefully this diminutive seamless *cache-coeur* will enhance your wardrobe like a bluebird instead of an *alouette*—with just a *soupçon* of color flittering around your shoulders. The silhouette is minimal, with gentle increases made as you approach the armholes. Then it's a straight shot (with a bit of side shaping) to the finish, followed by a picked-up ribbed hem and a sweet antique brooch or vintage button for closure.

One happy benefit of our French travels is discovering the fascinating flora and fauna of a region so unlike those of our watery home in Seattle. The colors of the area's wildlife alone are enough to send you on a beeline to the nearest yarn dyepot. From the gaudy pink, yet somehow strangely enticing (even for a pink-a-phobe like me) *flamants roses* (pink flamingos) quietly trolling the shallows in the sea's backwaters to the acid green lizards darting in and out of the midday shadows, I find, as Jane Austen would say, much to entertain. Alouette would be a perfect project to try a bolder color than you might commonly wear, since it does not overwhelm with its imprint. Sedate or bold, Alouette is indeed, *gentille*.

notes

Alouette is worked in rows from the top down, beginning with the decorative neck edging. Increases shape the yoke, then the sleeves are separated from the body, which continues down to the lower edge.

The neck circumference shown on the schematic includes the 1" (2.5 cm) ribbed bands at the front edges.

The shrug shown does not have a button closure. Directions for adding an optional button are given at the end of the finishing section.

shrug

NECK EDGING

With larger cir needle and using the cable method (see Glossary), CO 92 sts. Do not join in the rnd.

ROW 1: (RS) K1, yo, *k5, slip the second, third, fourth, and fifth st on the right needle tip over the first st, yo; rep from * to last st, k1—39 sts rem.

ROW 2: (WS) P1, *work (p1, yo, k1 through back loop) all in next st, p1; rep from *—77 sts.

ROW 3: K1, knit 1 through back loop (k1tbl), *k3, k1tbl; rep from * to last 3 sts, k3.

ROWS 4–6: Work even in St st (purl WS rows; knit RS rows) for 3 rows, beg and ending with a WS row—piece measures about 1½" (3.8 cm) from CO.

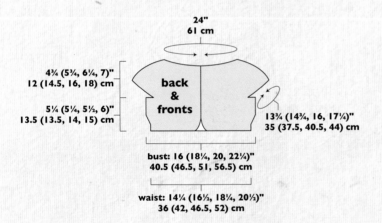

24"
61 cm

4¾ (5¾, 6¼, 7)"
12 (14.5, 16, 18) cm

back & fronts

5¼ (5¼, 5½, 6)"
13.5 (13.5, 14, 15) cm

13¾ (14¾, 16, 17¼)"
35 (37.5, 40.5, 44) cm

bust: 16 (18¼, 20, 22¼)"
40.5 (46.5, 51, 56.5) cm

waist: 14¼ (16½, 18¼, 20½)"
36 (42, 46.5, 52) cm

YOKE

Change to smaller cir needle.

ROW 7: (inc row) K7, work a lifted right-slant increase in next st on left needle tip, then knit the st itself (LRI; see Glossary), [k8, LRI] 7 times, k6—85 sts.

ROWS 8-10: Work even in St st.

ROW 11: (inc row): K6, LRI, [k7, LRI] 9 times, k6—95 sts.

ROWS 12-14: Work even in St st.

ROW 15: (inc row) K5, [k4, LRI] 17 times, k5—112 sts.

ROWS 16 AND 18: Purl.

ROW 17: (inc row) K2, LRI, [k8, LRI] 12 times, k1—125 sts.

ROW 19: (inc row) K2, LRI, [k4, LRI] 24 times, k2—150 sts.

ROWS 20-22: Work even in St st—piece measures 4¾" (12 cm) from CO.

Yoke shaping is complete for size 32"; skip to dividing row for this size. Cont for rem 3 sizes as foll:

ROW 23: (inc row) K5, LRI, [k5, LRI] 23 times, k6—174 sts.

ROWS 24-26: Work even in St st—piece measures 5¾" (14.5 cm) from CO.

Yoke shaping is complete for size 36½"; skip to dividing row for this size. Cont for rem 2 sizes as foll:

ROW 27: (inc row) K4, LRI, [k14, LRI] 11 times, k4—186 sts.

ROW 28: Purl—piece measures 6¼" (16 cm) from CO.

Yoke shaping is complete for size 40"; skip to dividing row for this size. Cont for size 44½" only as foll:

ROW 29: (inc row) K8, LRI, [k9, LRI] 17 times, k7—204 sts.

ROWS 30-32: Work even in St st—piece measures about 7" (18 cm) from CO.

DIVIDING ROW: (RS) K22 (25, 26, 28) for left front, place next 33 (37, 39, 41) sts on holder for left sleeve, use the backward-loop method (see Glossary) to CO 17 (17, 18, 19) sts, sl last CO st to left needle tip and work it tog with the st after it as k2tog, k39 (49, 55, 65) more sts for back (40 [50, 56, 66] back sts total), place next 33 (37, 39, 41) sts on holder for right sleeve, use the backward-loop method to CO 17 (17, 18, 19) sts, sl last CO st to left needle tip and work it tog with the st after it as k2tog, k21 (24, 25, 27) more sts for right front (22 [25, 26, 28] right front sts total)—116 (132, 142, 158) body sts rem.

LOWER BODY

Work 12 (12, 14, 16) rows even in St st, ending with a RS row—piece measures 2¾ (2¾, 3, 3½)" (7 [7, 7.5, 9] cm) from dividing row.

NEXT ROW: (WS) P30 (34, 36, 40), place marker (pm) for side "seam," p56 (64, 70, 78) back sts, pm for side "seam," p30 (34, 36, 40).

DEC ROW: (RS) Ssk, knit to 2 sts before m, ssk, slip marker (sl m), k2tog, work to 2 sts before next m, ssk, sl m, k2tog, work to last 2 sts, k2tog—6 sts dec'd; 2 sts each from back and each front.

[Work 1 WS row even, then rep the dec row] 2 times, then work 1 more WS row—98 (114, 124, 140) sts rem; 24 (28, 30, 34) sts each front; 50 (58, 64, 72) back sts; piece measures 4¼ (4¼, 4½, 5)" (11 [11, 11.5, 12.5] cm) from dividing row.

If adjusting length, work even in St st until lower body measures 1" (2.5 cm) less than desired total length (see Notes).

Leave sts on needle and cut yarn.

BODY EDGING

With RS facing, join yarn to CO row of left front neck edge. Using the right needle tip, pick up and knit 23 (25, 28, 32) sts along left front to sts on needle, picking up sts closer tog along shaping at bottom of left front to help ease the edging around the corner, then k98 (114, 124, 140) live sts on needle, then pick up and knit 23 (25, 28, 32) sts along left front, picking up sts closer tog along shaping at bottom of right front to ease edging around the corner and ending at CO row of right front neck edge—144 (164, 180, 204) sts total.

NEXT ROW: (WS) K1, *p2, k2; rep from * to last 3 sts, p2, k1.

NEXT ROW: (RS) P1, *k2, p2; rep from * to last 3 sts, k2, p1.

Rep the last 2 rows once more—piece measures 5¼ (5¼, 5½, 6)" (13.5 [13.5, 14, 15] cm) from dividing row.

Loosely BO all sts in rib patt.

sleeves

Place 33 (37, 39, 41) held sleeve sts on 3 dpn. With RS facing, join yarn to beg of sts BO at underarm, pick up and knit 17 (17, 19, 21) sts across underarm BO sts, sl last picked-up st to left needle tip, pm on right needle to indicate beg of rnd, work transferred picked-up st tog with the first sleeve st after it as k2tog, k31 (35, 37, 39) sleeve sts, work the last sleeve st tog with the picked-up st after it as k2tog, then k15 (15, 17, 19) rem picked-up sts again to end at m—48 (52, 56, 60) sts.

Redistribute sts as evenly as possible on 3 or 4 dpn and join for working in rnds. If adjusting sleeve length, work even in St st until sleeve measures ¾" (2 cm) less than desired.

NEXT RND: *K2, p2; rep from *.

Rep the last rnd 2 more times—sleeve measures ¾" (2 cm) from dividing rnd. BO all sts loosely in rib patt.

finishing

Wet-block (see Glossary) to ease ribbed edging around the lower front corners and to open up the neck edging.

Weave in loose ends.

OPTIONAL BUTTON CLOSURE

Sew button to right neck about 1" (2.5 cm) in from center front edge and 1" (2.5) cm down from neck CO, with button backing fabric held on WS beneath button for reinforcement, and sewing through both the shrug and the backing fabric layers. With crochet hook, attach a 12" (30.5 cm) length of yarn to the left front edge about 1" (2.5 cm) down from neck CO. Work a crochet chain (see Glossary) about 6" (15 cm) long, then fasten off last st. To close shrug, wrap chain around button shank and tie in place.

FINISHED SIZE

About 20" (51 cm) wide and 54" (137 cm) long.

YARN

Lace weight (#0 Lace).

SHOWN HERE: Shibui Knits Silk Cloud (60% kid mohair, 40% silk; 330 yd [300 m]/25 g): #2001 abyss (black), 2 skeins.

Habu Textiles A-20 Silk/Stainless Steel (69% silk, 31% stainless steel; 311 yd [284 m]/½ oz [14 g]): #2 black, 2 cones.

NEEDLES

Size U.S. 11 (8 mm): two 32" (80 cm) or longer circular (cir).

Adjust needle size if necessary to obtain the correct gauge.

NOTIONS

Markers (m); tapestry needle.

GAUGE

17 sts and 32 rows of ostrich plume panel measure 4" (10 cm) wide and 7" (18 cm) high using one strand of each yarn held tog, after blocking.

15 sts of stockinette panel measure 4" (10 cm) wide using one strand of each yarn held tog, after blocking.

tattoo

SHAWL

Like an inky scroll of body art, Tattoo stretches across bare shoulders for the perfect modern wrap that exudes high fashion with a dose of French gothic mystique. Worked in a duo of spider-web–thin silk wrapped around stainless steel and silk-rich mohair, an ostrich-plume–stitch pattern is dissected and reassembled with panels of stockinette that lighten the lace and give the design a contemporary edge.

I do not wear shawls anymore. This is coming from someone who has lived and worked (labored, to be exact—I was wrapped in one of my hand-made crocheted shawls when I gave birth to my son) and played in every kind of wrap under the sun. I must have craved a change, because the closest I would get to one today would be an *étole* exactly like Tattoo.

So, if you're feeling in a rectangular sort of mood (and I hope you are), this little lovely works up quite happily in two halves knitted simultaneously, then after a quick bit of Kitchener stitch to join them, *voilà, c'est fini!*

notes

Tattoo is worked with one strand of each yarn held together throughout. Adding the stainless-steel-core yarn helps the fabric hold its shape better than the silk/mohair yarn alone, and it's much easier to recover the stitches if the work slips off the needles or if you need to correct a mistake.

This project is constructed in two halves. Each half begins by working five individual scallops that are joined across, and then the stitches are worked in pattern to the center. During finishing, the two halves are grafted along the center line.

Although you may work each half separately, I encourage you to work both halves at the same time, side by side on a long needle using separate yarn for each half. You may find it easier to keep track of rows this way, and your tension will be consistent in both halves.

To adjust the length, work more or fewer repeats of the 32-row ostrich-plume panel. Every repeat added or removed will lengthen or shorten the shawl by about 14" (35.5 cm) when the same 32-row adjustment is made in both halves. Plan on purchasing extra yarn if making a longer shawl.

stitch guide

Ostrich-Plume Panel (worked over 17 sts)

ROW 1: (RS) [K1, yo] 3 times, [ssk] 2 times, [sl 2, k1, p2sso], [k2tog] 2 times, [yo, k1] 3 times.

ROWS 2–4: Work 3 rows even in St st.

ROWS 5–16: Rep Rows 1–4 three times.

ROW 17: [K2tog] 3 times, [yo, k1] 5 times, yo, [ssk] 3 times.

ROWS 18–20: Work 3 rows even in St st.

ROWS 21–32: Rep Rows 17–20 three times.

Rep Rows 1–32 for patt.

edging

Using the cable method (see Glossary), CO 17 sts. Work Rows 1–6 of ostrich-plume panel (see Stitch Guide) once. Place sts on holder. Make 4 more scallops in the same manner, but leave the fifth scallop on the needle and do not cut yarn—17 sts from fifth scallop rem on needle.

JOIN SCALLOPS

With RS facing, place four held scallops on needle so that the fifth scallop with the working yarn attached will be worked first—85 sts total on needle.

JOINING ROW: (RS) K16, k2tog, place marker (pm), k15, pm, k2tog, k15, k2tog, pm, k15, pm, k2tog, k16—81 sts rem.

Cont for working your method as foll:

For working each half separately
Purl 1 WS row, then skip to the Body section.

For working two halves side by side (see Notes)

Use the second cir needle to make another five scallops as before, leaving the fifth scallop on the second needle; do not cut yarn. With RS facing, place four held scallops on needle so that the fifth scallop with the working yarn attached will be worked first—85 sts on second cir needle. With RS facing and using yarn attached to first scallop on the second needle, work the second set of scallops onto the end of the first cir needle by working the joining row across them—two groups of 81 sts on one cir needle. Purl 1 WS row, working each half with its own yarn. From now on, take care that you do not accidentally join the two pieces by working across both halves using the same yarn.

body

NOTE: *If working both halves at the same time on one needle, work each instruction across the first half, then work the instruction again across the second half.*

Beg with Row 5 of patt (Rows 1–4 are deliberately not worked at the start of the body), establish St st and ostrich-plume panels (see Stitch Guide) as foll:

SET-UP ROW: (RS) *Work Row 5 of ostrich-plume panel over 17 sts, sl m, work 15 sts in St st, sl m; rep from * once more, work Row 5 of ostrich-plume panel over last 17 sts.

Working 17-st sections in ostrich-plume patt as established and 15-st sections in St st, work Rows 6–32 of patt once, then work Rows 1–32 of patt 2 times, or as many times as needed for the desired length (see Notes).

Removing markers as you come to them in the first row, work lace patt across all sts as foll:

ROW 1: (RS) *[K1, yo] 3 times, [ssk] 2 times, sl 2 tog knitwise, k1, p2sso, [k2tog] 2 times, [yo, k1] 2 times, yo; rep from * to last st, k1.

ROWS 2–4: Work 3 rows even in St st.

Rep Rows 1–4 five more times.

Cont for your method of working as foll:

For working each half separately

Cut yarn and set first half aside. Use the second cir needle to make a second half in the same manner, then cut yarn leaving a tail about 3 times the width of the shawl for grafting—81 sts each on two needles.

For working two halves side by side

Cut yarns, leaving a tail about 3 times the width of the pieces attached to one half for grafting. Transfer the 81 sts of one half to the second cir needle—81 sts each on two needles.

finishing

With tail threaded on a tapestry needle, use the Kitchener st for St st (see Glossary) to graft the two halves together, taking care to match the tension of the lace fabric.

Weave in loose ends.

Wet-block (see Glossary) to about 20" (51 cm) wide and 54" (137 cm) long, pinning the scalloped edges into gentle curves.

FINISHED SIZE

About 19¼" (49 cm) wide and 52" (132 cm) long, after blocking, but before tucks. With selvedges allowed to roll, piece will measure about 18" (45.5 cm) wide.

YARN

Fingering weight (#1 Super Fine).

SHOWN HERE: Rowan Kidsilk Haze (70% kid mohair, 30% silk; 229 yd [210 m]/25 g): #578 swish (gold), 2 balls.

NOTE: *The color shown has been discontinued; substitute the color of your choice.*

NEEDLES

Size U.S. 8 (5 mm): two 24" (60 cm) circular (cir).

Adjust needle size if necessary to obtain the correct gauge.

NOTIONS

Removable markers; tapestry needle.

GAUGE

17 sts and 17 rows = 4" (10 cm) in St st, after blocking.

safran
SHRUG

Near the French-Spanish border, where the Pyrenees tumble dramatically toward the sea, the quintessential picture-postcard fishing port of Collioure has been a favorite destination since my early days in France. An object of tug-of-war between the two warring countries for centuries and now firmly settled in France, the region has profited from years of political unrest, developing a culinary mélange that encompasses southern French, Catalan, North African, and Spanish flavors. There, on an uncharacteristically rain-soaked evening, I tasted my first *Soupe de Poisson*— a peasant dish born of frugally using bits of trimmings from the day's catch. The savory broth supports crisp rounds of day-old baguette crowned with dollops of saffron-infused *rouille* (spicy olive-oil mayonnaise) and shredded Parmesan—for me, it was love at first taste and the beginning of a quest for authentic rural French recipes that I could experiment with in my home kitchen. The ochre-tinted broth of this dreamy dish is the exact color I envisioned when I designed Safran—a *soufflé* of Rowan Kidsilk Haze swirled around the shoulders with strategic tiny tucks to fold it into an airy shrug. The ultimate mindless stockinette project at the outset, origami-like pleats are added after blocking, then Kitchener stitch closes the oval, and a tiny seam at the back forms the sleeve openings . . . *c'est façile!*

notes

Refer to the sidebar below for tips on working with silk/mohair yarn. Keeping even tension during the knitting and the Kitchener stitch join is paramount to success.

FOR THE LOVE OF SILK/MOHAIR YARN

Here are some tips for working with this little beauty:

Though most yarn of this type is put up in pull balls or skeins, take time to roll it into balls.

Place the wound ball inside a small ziplock bag and "zip" all but an inch of the top so the yarn can feed through freely. This keeps the yarn clean and tangle-free and works especially well if you're working with multiple strands of yarn (either double strands of silk/mohair or silk/mohair plus another yarn).

To deal with a mistake that is difficult to rip back, or if your work has fallen off your needles, place the entire piece along with the working yarn in a large ziplock bag, then place it in the freezer for 10 minutes or so until the fibers firm up but not so long that ice crystals form. The cold fiber will be easier to detangle or replace on the needles.

Use a lifeline if you are concerned about the stitches slipping off the needles. Periodically (say, at the end of each pattern repeat) draw a tapestry needle threaded with a strand of thin smooth yarn or dental floss through the stitches on the needle. On the next row, take care not catch the lifeline into the knitting. If you do make a mistake, simply ravel to the lifeline. If you use a set of interchangeable needles, thread dental floss into the hole at the base of the needle and knit a row as usual—the lifeline will be added as you knit (I learned this tip from www.knittinghelp.com).

shrug

Using the invisible method and substituting a second cir needle for the waste yarn (see sidebar on page 23), CO 82 sts.

Work even in St st (knit RS rows; purl WS rows) until piece measures 52½" (133.5 cm) from CO. Cut yarn, leaving a 60" (152.5 cm) tail to use for grafting later. Leave sts on needle.

finishing

With cir needles in place as holders at each end of piece, wet-block (see Glossary) piece to 19¼" (49 cm) wide and 52½" (133.5 cm) long, using blocking wires on long edges if desired. Allow to air-dry thoroughly.

TUCKS

For the first set of tucks, find the centerline of the St st rectangle—41 sts on each side of center. Mark a series of tucks along this centerline as foll: Beg at end with the last row of sts worked, measure down 3¾" (9.5 cm) from the cir needle holder and place a removable marker (m) directly in the fabric, [then measure down 7½" (19 cm) directly below the previous m and place a removable m in the fabric] 6 times—7 markers along centerline; the top and bottom m are each 3¾" (9.5 cm) from the end of the fabric.

For the second and third sets of tucks, count in 10 sts from the selvedge along each long side. Mark a series of tucks along the line at each side, 10 sts from the selvedge, as foll: Beg at end with the last row of sts worked, measure down 7½" (19 cm) from the cir needle holder and place a removable m directly in the fabric, [then measure down 7½" (19 cm) from previous m and place a removable m in the fabric] 6 times—14 side markers total; 7 markers at each side placed 10 sts in from the edge; the bottom m at each side is just above the needle holding the provisional CO sts.

To sew the center tucks, thread a length of yarn on a tapestry needle and anchor it securely to the WS at a marked centerline position. With RS of fabric facing you, bring the needle up through the fabric from WS to RS 7 sts to the left of the marked position. Skim the needle through the st that is 7 sts to the left of the marked position, then through the st at the marker, then through the st that is 7 sts to the right of the marked position—3 sts caught on the tucking strand. Pull strand to draw the 3 sts tog, then sew through all 3 sts again 8 to 10 times using an overhand st. Fasten yarn invisibly on WS under the tuck. Work a center tuck at each of the rem 6 marked centerline positions.

To sew the side tucks along the right-hand edge of the fabric, thread a length of yarn on a tapestry needle and anchor it securely to the WS at a marked position. With RS of fabric facing you, bring the needle up through the fabric from WS to RS 10 sts to the left of the marked position. Skim the needle through the st that is 10 sts to the left of the marked position, then through the st at the marker, then through the selvedge st that is 10 sts to the right of the marked position—3 sts caught on the tucking strand. Finish as for center tuck. Work a tuck at each of the rem 6 marked positions along the right-hand edge of the fabric.

To sew the side tucks along the left-hand edge of the fabric, thread a length of yarn on a tapestry needle and anchor it securely to the WS at a marked position. With RS of fabric facing you, bring the needle up through the fabric from WS to RS 10 sts to the right of the marked position. Skim the needle through the st that is 10 sts to the right of the marked position, then through the st at the marker, then through the selvedge st that is 10 sts to the left of the marked position—3 sts caught on the tucking strand. Finish as for center tuck. Work a tuck at each of the rem 6 marked positions along the left-hand edge of the fabric.

JOIN SHORT ENDS

Hold cir needles parallel with WS touching and RS facing out, being careful not to twist piece. Use the Kitchener st for St st (see Glossary) to graft the live sts at the ends tog.

BACK SEAM

Lay piece flat with selvedges running horizontally across the top and bottom and the Kitchener join positioned vertically in the center of the side facing you. Measure out 4½" (11.5 cm) on each side of the join along the top edges and pin both layers tog at these points. With yarn threaded on a tapestry needle, use the mattress st (see Glossary) to sew the two layers tog between the marked points. There will be about 8½" (21.5 cm) left unsewn at each side of the top edge; these unsewn sections form the armholes.

Weave in loose ends.

FINISHED SIZE

About 36¼" (92 cm) long from center top of head to base of cowl, measured along cabled front edge.

YARN

Chunky (#5 Bulky).

SHOWN HERE: Louisa Harding Rossetti (67% merino, 28% silk, 5% nylon; 76 yd [69 m]/50 g); #8 coal (dark blue), 6 skeins.

NEEDLES

Size U.S. 10 (6 mm): 24" (60 cm) or longer circular (cir).

Adjust needle size if necessary to obtain the correct gauge.

NOTIONS

Smooth cotton yarn for provisional cast-on; markers (m); removable marker; stitch holders; spare needles same size or smaller than main needle to hold sts for grafting; tapestry needle.

GAUGE

12 sts and 22 rows = 4" (10 cm) in garter stitch.

14 sts of Cable chart measure 2½" (6.5 cm) at widest point, 19 rows of chart measure 4" (10 cm) high.

morgaine

HOODED COWL

My earliest memories are aromatic—the honeyed sweet pea blossoms in the family garden, the salty seaweed scent of my bayside childhood cottage, the deep fern glen and balsam cedar permeating our forest hideaways. It is no surprise that I have always stirred up perfumed potions and aligned myself with conjurers of the past from mysterious cultures a world away from my tranquil woodland youth. Recalling that first brush with the Arthurian legends as I read and reread the worn pages of my grandfather's leather-bound volumes, I knew I had found a passion. I felt more kinship to the supposedly wicked Morgana (or as she is called in French, Morgan le Fay, from *la fée*—Morgan of the Fairies), and was enthralled by her mandrake root and prescient visions. In a world before *Harry Potter* and *Twilight*, this was the stuff of dreams for a ten-year-old.

It was a great relief to read another accounting of that story years later in *The Mists of Avalon* by Marion Zimmer Bradley, which shed a more feminine light on the tale.

Be she devil or angel, Morgaine made a strong impression, and I had her character deeply in mind when I designed this cowl/hood that can preserve any wanderer against the damp and cold. Short-rows shape the curving garter-stitch body of the garment that sprouts from stitches picked up along the edge of the long, loose cable edging. And like the hue of Morgaine's cloak, the soft, shimmering deep indigo yarn from Louisa Harding forms a halo of loveliness around the face.

notes

If desired, use the cable portion of a spare circular needle in place of waste yarn when working the provisional cast-on (see sidebar on page 23).

The cable edging is worked a deliberately tighter gauge than is suggested on the ball band. Take care to swatch the cable pattern before you begin and work the edging using a smaller needle if necessary to achieve the correct gauge.

The first time you work Row 1 of the Cable chart, work the first stitch as k1. On all following repeats, slip the first stitch of Row 1 as if to purl with yarn in back (pwise wyb) as shown on the chart.

In Rows 10–16 of the Cable chart, the purl columns (as they appear from the RS) deliberately do not contain any p2tog, yo lace patterning.

stitch guide

14-st Rib Cable: SI 6 sts onto cable needle (cn) and hold in front of work, [k2, p2] 2 times, then work 6 sts from cn as k2, p2, k2.

NOTE: *When you work the first 8 cable sts you will be knitting the purls and purling the knits as they appear; this is necessary to maintain a knit column along the front edge at the start of the row.*

cable edging

Using a provisional method and the cable portion of a spare cir needle (see sidebar on page 23), CO 14 sts. Knitting the first st the first time you work Row 1 (see Notes), work Rows 1–32 of Cable chart 5 times, then work Rows 1–13 once more—173 rows completed. With RS facing, place a removable marker at the end of the last row to indicate center of edging for picking up sts later. Work Rows 14–32 once, work Rows 1–32 four times, then work Rows 1–25 once more, ending with a RS row—172 rows from marked row in center; 345 rows total; piece measures 72½" (184 cm) from CO and about 36¼" (92 cm) from marked row.

CABLE

□		knit on RS; purl on WS
•		purl on RS; knit on WS
o		yo
✗		p2tog
v		sl 1 pwise wyb on RS and WS
⤬		14-st rib cable (see Stitch Guide)

hood and cowl

With RS still facing, hold edging horizontally with long edge at end of RS rows running across the top and live sts on needle to your right. With RS facing, pick up and knit 91 sts evenly spaced along selvedge of edging to marked row, discard removable marker, place regular stitch marker (m) on needle, pick up and knit 91 sts evenly spaced to CO, remove waste yarn from provisional CO, place 14 sts from base of CO on needle, and knit across them—210 sts total; 182 picked-up sts and 14 sts from ends of edging at each side.

Work short-rows to shape hood as foll:

ROW 1: (WS) Knit to center m, slip marker (sl m), k16, turn work.

ROW 2: (RS) Yo, k16, sl m, k16, turn work—32 sts between turning gaps.

Sl center m on all foll rows as you come to it.

ROWS 3 AND 4: Yo, knit to yo of previous row, work yo tog with next st after it as k2tog, k3, turn.

ROWS 5–22: Rep Rows 3 and 4 nine more times—112 sts between turning gaps.

ROWS 23 AND 24: Yo, knit to yo of previous row, work yo tog with next st after it as k2tog, knit to last 3 sts at end of row, turn.

ROWS 25 AND 26: Yo, knit to 2 sts before yo at turning gap, turn.

ROWS 27–54: Rep Rows 25 and 26 fourteen more times—16 turning gaps with yo's at each side.

ROWS 55 AND 56: Knit to end, working each yo tog with st after it as k2tog when you come to it.

ROW 57: Knit 1 WS row across all sts—piece measures 10¼" (26 cm) from pick-up row at center.

Cut yarn, leaving a 24" (61 cm) tail for grafting.

finishing

Place the first 15 and the last 15 sts of row on separate spare needles for grafting—180 center sts rem on main needle. Hold sts on grafting needles tog with WS touching and RS facing out, making sure the piece is not twisted. Thread tail on a tapestry needle and use the Kitchener st for St st (see Glossary) to graft sts tog to join flaps at bottom of cowl.

Place 30 sts on each side of center m on separate spare needles for grafting—60 sts rem on main needle on each side of center sts. Hold sts on grafting needles tog with WS touching and RS facing out. Using a separate strand of yarn and Kitchener st, graft center sts tog for "seam" at back of hood.

With RS facing, rejoin yarn to first group of 60 sts on main needle, ready to work a RS row. BO rem sts while picking up and binding off extra sts at base of grafted seam to reinforce nape of neck as foll: (RS) BO first 60 live sts to hood seam, [pick up and knit 1 st from selvedge, BO 1 st] 8 times, BO rem 60 live sts.

Weave in loose ends. Wet-block (see Glossary) to measurements, pinning cable edging into gentle curves as shown.

glossary

ABBREVIATIONS

beg(s)	begin(s); beginning	M1	make one (increase)	tbl	through back loop
BO	bind off	p	purl	tog	together
CC	contrasting color	p1f&b	purl into front and back of same stitch	WS	wrong side
cir	circular			wyb	with yarn in back
cm	centimeter(s)	patt(s)	pattern(s)	wyf	with yarn in front
cn	cable needle	psso	pass slipped stitch over	yd	yard(s)
CO	cast on	pwise	purlwise, as if to purl	yo	yarnover
cont	continue(s); continuing	rem	remain(s); remaining	*	repeat starting point
dec(s)	decrease(s); decreasing	rep	repeat(s); repeating	**	repeat all instructions between asterisks
dpn	double-pointed needles	rev St st	reverse stockinette stitch		
foll	follow(s); following	rnd(s)	round(s)	( )	alternate measurements and/or instructions
g	gram(s)	RS	right side		
inc(s)	increase(s); increasing	sl	slip	[ ]	work instructions as a group a specified number of times
k	knit	sl st	slip st (slip 1 stitch purlwise unless otherwise indicated)		
k1f&b	knit into the front and back of same stitch				
kwise	knitwise, as if to knit	ssk	slip, slip, knit		
m	marker(s)	ssp	slip, slip, purl		
MC	main color	st(s)	stitch(es)		
mm	millimeter(s)	St st	stockinette stitch		

bind-offs

DECREASE BIND-OFF

Slip the first stitch, knit the second stitch, then *knit these two stitches together by inserting the left needle tip into the front of both from left to right (**Figure 1**) and knitting them together through their back loops. Knit the next stitch (**Figure 2**). Repeat from * for the desired number of stitches.

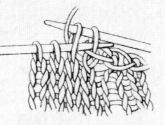

figure 1

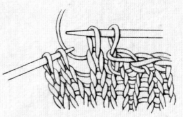

figure 2

JENY'S SURPRISINGLY STRETCHY BIND-OFF

To Collar a Knit Stitch: Bring working yarn from back to front over needle in the opposite direction of a normal yarnover (**Figure 1**), knit the next stitch, then lift the yarnover over the top of the knitted stitch and off the needle (**Figure 2**).

To Collar a Purl Stitch: Bring working yarn from front to back over needle as for a normal yarnover (**Figure 3**), purl the next stitch, then lift the yarnover over the top of the purled stitch and off the needle (**Figure 4**).

To begin, collar each of the first two stitches to match their knit or purl nature. Then pass the first collared stitch over the second and off the right needle—one stitch is bound off.

*Collar the next stitch according to its nature (**Figure 5**), then pass the previous stitch over the collared stitch and off the needle (**Figure 6**).

Repeat from * until one stitch remains on the right needle. Cut the yarn, leaving a 6″ (15 cm) tail, then pull on the loop of the last stitch until the tail comes free.

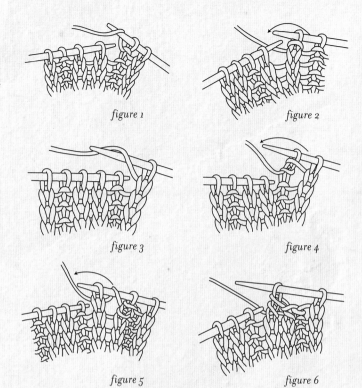

figure 1

figure 2

figure 3

figure 4

figure 5

figure 6

SEWN BIND-OFF

Cut the yarn, leaving a tail about four times the length of the edge of the knitting to be bound off, and thread the tail onto a tapestry needle.

Working from right to left, *insert tapestry needle purlwise (from right to left) through the first two stitches (**Figure 1**) and pull the yarn through.

Bring tapestry needle knitwise (from left to right) through the first stitch (**Figure 2**), pull the yarn through, then slip this stitch off the knitting needle.

Repeat from * for the desired number of stitches.

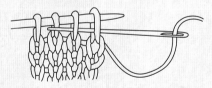

figure 1

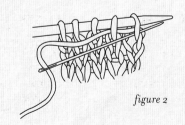

figure 2

blocking

WET-BLOCKING

Place a few drops or so of mild wool wash in sink or large container and fill with cool water. Add garment and let soak for about 30 minutes, making sure that it becomes completely saturated. Remove from basin carefully, supporting entire weight, squeeze very gently, and lay flat on large, clean towel. Roll in towel and press to remove excess water. Lay garment flat on dry towels or blocking board away from direct sunlight and shape to desired dimensions, pinning out delicate details such as the points in lace. Allow to air-dry thoroughly.

cast-ons

BACKWARD-LOOP CAST-ON

*Loop working yarn and place it on needle backward so that it doesn't unwind. Repeat from *.

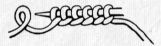

CABLE CAST-ON

If there are no stitches on the needles, make a slipknot of working yarn and place it on the needle, then use the knitted method to cast-on one more stitch—two stitches on needle. Hold needle with working yarn in your left hand. *Insert right needle between the first two stitches on left needle (**Figure 1**), wrap yarn around needle as if to knit, draw yarn through (**Figure 2**), and place new loop on left needle (**Figure 3**) to form a new stitch. Repeat from * for the desired number of stitches, always working between the first two stitches on the left needle.

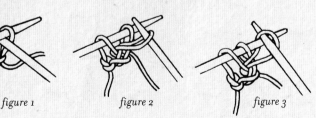

figure 1   *figure 2*   *figure 3*

EMILY OCKER'S CIRCULAR CAST-ON

Leaving a 6" (15 cm) tail, twist the working yarn into a circle so that the cross is at the top and the tail goes to the left. With a double-pointed needle, *reach inside the loop and pull the working yarn through to make a stitch, then bring the needle up over the top of the loop and make a yarnover; repeat from * for the desired number of stitches. Turn the work and knit one row, then divide the stitches onto separate needles for working in rounds. During finishing, pull the starting tail to close the center hole.

NOTE: *If desired, you can use a crochet hook instead and work the desired number of a series of single crochets around the circle, keeping the loops on the hook as you work.*

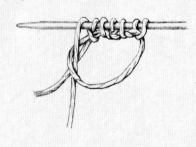

INVISIBLE PROVISIONAL CAST-ON

Make a loose slipknot of working yarn and place it on the right needle. Hold a length of contrasting waste yarn (of the cable part of a circular needle; see page 23) next to the slipknot and around your left thumb; hold working yarn over your left index finger. *Bring the right needle forward, then under waste yarn, over working yarn, grab a loop of working yarn and bring it forward under working yarn (**Figure 1**), then bring needle back behind the working yarn and grab a second loop (**Figure 2**). Repeat from * for the desired number of stitches. When you're ready to work in the opposite direction, place the exposed loops on a knitting needle as you pull out the waste yarn.

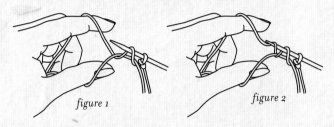

figure 1   *figure 2*

KNITTED CAST-ON

Make a slipknot of working yarn and place it on the left needle if there are no stitches already there. *Use the right needle to knit the first stitch (or slipknot) on left needle (**Figure 1**) and place new loop onto left needle to form a new stitch (**Figure 2**). Repeat from * for the desired number of stitches, always working into the last stitch made.

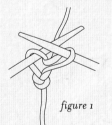 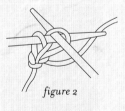

figure 1   *figure 2*

LONG-TAIL (CONTINENTAL) CAST-ON

Leaving a long tail (about ½" [1.3 cm] for each stitch to be cast on), make a slipknot and place it on the right needle.

Place the thumb and index finger of your left hand between the yarn ends so that the working yarn is around your index finger and the tail end is around your thumb. Secure both yarn ends with your other fingers. Hold your palm upward, making a V of yarn (**Figure 1**).

*Bring the needle up through the loop on your thumb (**Figure 2**), catch the first strand around your index finger, and bring the needle back down through the loop on your thumb (**Figure 3**).

Drop the loop off your thumb and place your thumb back in the V configuration while tightening the resulting stitch on the needle (**Figure 4**).

Repeat from * for the desired number of stitches.

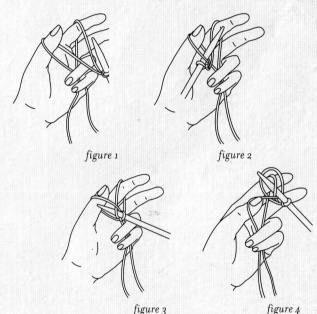

figure 1   *figure 2*

figure 3   *figure 4*

crochet

CROCHET CHAIN (CH)

Make a slipknot and place it on crochet hook if there isn't a loop already on the hook. *Yarn over hook and draw through loop on hook. Repeat from * for the desired number of stitches. To fasten off, cut yarn and draw end through last loop formed.

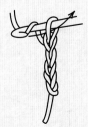

decreases

SLIP, SLIP, KNIT (SSK)

Slip two stitches individually knitwise (**Figure 1**), insert left needle tip into the front of these two slipped stitches, and use the right needle to knit them together through their back loops (**Figure 2**).

SLIP, SLIP, PURL (SSP)

Holding yarn in front, slip two stitches individually knitwise (**Figure 1**), then slip these two stitches back onto left needle (they will be turned on the needle) and purl them together through their back loops (**Figure 2**).

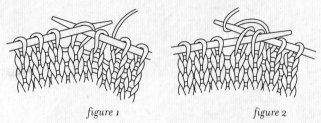

figure 1   *figure 2*

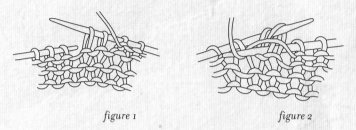

figure 1   *figure 2*

SLIP, SLIP, SLIP, KNIT (SSSK)

Slip three stitches individually knitwise, insert left needle tip into the front of these three slipped stitches, and use the right needle to knit them together through their back loops.

grafting

KITCHENER STITCH FOR STOCKINETTE STITCH

Arrange stitches on two needles so that there is the same number of stitches on each needle. Hold the needles parallel to each other with wrong sides of the knitting together. Allowing about ½" (1.3 cm) per stitch to be grafted, thread matching yarn on a tapestry needle. Work from right to left as follows:

STEP 1. Bring tapestry needle through the first stitch on the front needle as if to purl and leave the stitch on the needle (**Figure 1**).

STEP 2. Bring tapestry needle through the first stitch on the back needle as if to knit and leave that stitch on the needle (**Figure 2**).

STEP 3. Bring tapestry needle through the first front stitch as if to knit and slip this stitch off the needle, then bring tapestry needle through the next front stitch as if to purl and leave this stitch on the needle (**Figure 3**).

STEP 4. Bring tapestry needle through the first back stitch as if to purl and slip this stitch off the needle, then bring tapestry needle through the next back stitch as if to knit and leave this stitch on the needle (**Figure 4**).

Repeat Steps 3 and 4 until one stitch remains on each needle, adjusting the tension to match the rest of the knitting as you go. To finish, bring tapestry needle through the front stitch as if to knit and slip this stitch off the needle, then bring tapestry needle through the back stitch as if to purl and slip this stitch off the needle.

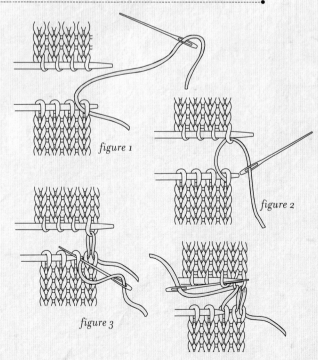

figure 1

figure 2

figure 3

figure 4

KITCHENER STITCH FOR GARTER STITCH

End the knitting so that one piece ends with a right-side row (knit stitches just below the needles when viewed from the right side) and the other piece ends with a wrong-side row (purl stitches just below the needles when viewed from the right side). Hold the needles parallel to each other with the piece that ended with a wrong-side row on the top and the piece that ended with a right-side row on the bottom and so that the working yarn is at the right tips of the needles. Allowing about ½" (1.3 cm) per stitch to be grafted, thread matching yarn on a tapestry needle. Work from right to left as follows:

STEP 1. Bring tapestry needle through the first stitch on the lower needle as if to knit, then through the first stitch on the upper needle as if to purl (**Figure 1**).

STEP 2. Bring tapestry needle through the first stitch on the lower needle (the stitch entered in Step 1) as if to purl and slip this stitch off the needle, then through the next stitch as if to knit (**Figure 2**) and leave this stitch on the needle.

STEP 3. Bring tapestry needle through the first stitch on the upper needle (the stitch entered in Step 1) as if to knit and slip this stitch off the needle, then through the next stitch as if to purl (**Figure 3**) and leave this stitch on the needle.

Repeat Steps 2 and 3, adjusting the tension to match the rest of the knitting as you go and ending by bringing the tapestry needle purlwise through the last stitch on the lower needle, then knitwise through the last stitch on the upper needle (**Figure 4**).

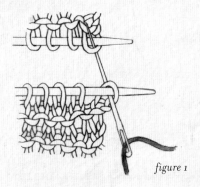

figure 1

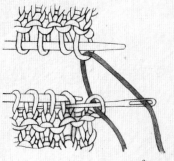

figure 2

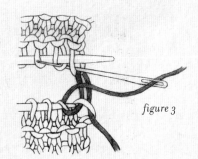

figure 3

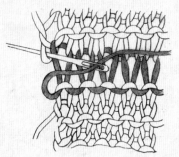

figure 4

increases

BAR INCREASE—KNITWISE (K1F&B)

Knit into a stitch but leave it on the left needle (**Figure 1**), then knit through the back loop of the same stitch (**Figure 2**) and slip the original stitch off the needle (**Figure 3**).

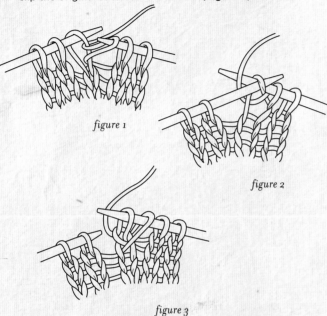

figure 1

figure 2

figure 3

BAR INCREASE—PURLWISE (P1F&B)

Purl into a stitch but leave it on the left needle (**Figure 1**), then purl through the back loop of the same stitch (**Figure 2**) and slip the original stitch off the needle.

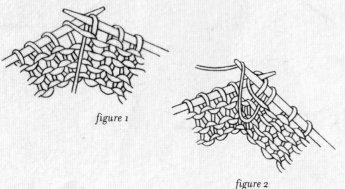

figure 1

figure 2

RAISED MAKE-ONE (M1)

With left needle tip, lift the strand between the last knitted stitch and the first stitch on the left needle from front to back (Figure 1), then knit the lifted loop through the back.

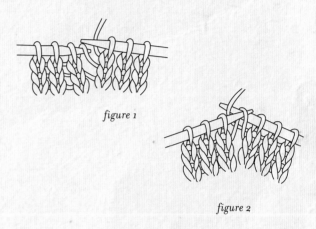

figure 1

figure 2

RAISED MAKE-ONE PURLWISE (M1P)

With left needle tip, lift the strand between the needles from front to back (Figure 1), then purl the lifted loop through the back (Figure 2).

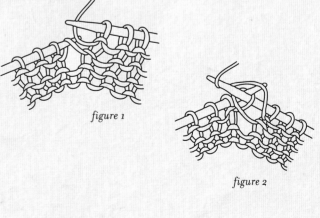

figure 1

figure 2

LIFTED INCREASE—LEFT SLANT (LLI)

Insert left needle tip into the back of the stitch below the stitch just knitted (**Figure 1**), then knit this stitch (**Figure 2**).

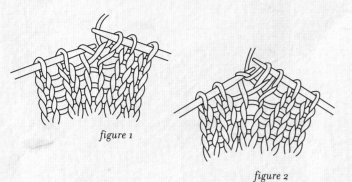

figure 1

figure 2

LIFTED INCREASE—RIGHT SLANT (LRI)

Knit into the back of the stitch (in the "purl bump") in the row directly below the stitch on the left needle (**Figure 1**), then knit the stitch on the needle (**Figure 2**), and slip the original stitch off the needle.

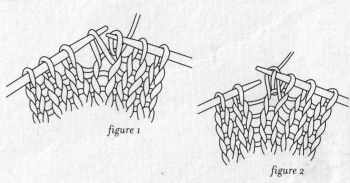

figure 1

figure 2

running stitch

Bring threaded needle in and out of background to form a dashed line.

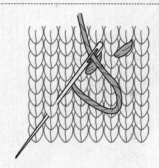

seams

MATTRESS STITCH

Place the pieces to be seamed on a table, right sides facing up. Begin at the lower edge and work upward as follows for your stitch pattern:

Stockinette Stitch with 1-Stitch Seam Allowance

Insert threaded needle under one bar between the two edge stitches on one piece, then under the corresponding bar plus the bar above it on the other piece (**Figure 1**). *Pick up the next two bars on the first piece (**Figure 2**), then the next two bars on the other (**Figure 3**). Repeat from *, ending by picking up the last bar or pair of bars on the first piece.

Stockinette Stitch with ½-Stitch Seam Allowance

To reduce bulk in the mattress-stitch seam, work as for the 1-stitch seam allowance but pick up the bars in the center of the edge stitches instead of between the last two stitches.

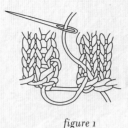 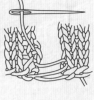 

figure 1   *figure 2*   *figure 3*

tassel

Cut a piece of cardboard 4″ (10 cm) wide by the desired length of the tassel plus 1″ (2.5 cm). Wrap yarn to desired thickness around cardboard. Cut a short length of yarn and tie tightly around one end of wrapped yarn (**Figure 1**). Cut yarn loops at other end. Cut another piece of yarn and wrap tightly around loops a short distance below top knot to form tassel neck. Knot securely, thread ends onto tapestry needle, and pull to center of tassel (**Figure 2**). Trim ends.

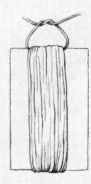 

figure 1   *figure 2*

twisted cord

Cut several lengths of yarn about five times the desired finished cord length. Fold the strands in half to form two equal groups. Anchor the strands at the fold by looping them over a doorknob. Holding one group in each hand, twist each group tightly in a clockwise direction until they begin to kink. Put both groups in one hand, then release them, allowing them to twist around each other counterclockwise. Smooth out the twists so that they are uniform along the length of the cord. Knot the ends.

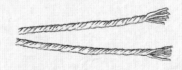

sources for yarn

BERROCO INC.

1 Tupperware Dr., Ste. 4
North Smithfield, RI 02896
Berroco.com
In Canada: Westminster Fibers (Canada)

BLUE SKY ALPACAS

PO Box 88
Cedar, MN 55011
blueskyalpacas.com

DIAMOND YARN

9697 Blvd. St. Laurent, Ste. Porte 101
Montreal, QC
Canada H3L 2N1
and
155 Martin Ross Ave., Unit 3
Toronto, ON
Canada M3J 2L9
diamondyarn.com

HABU TEXTILES

135 W. 29th St., Ste. 804
New York, NY 10001
habutextiles.com

**KNITTING FEVER INC./
LOUISA HARDING**

PO Box 336
315 Bayview Ave.
Amityville, NY 11701
knittingfever.com
In Canada: Diamond Yarn

QUINCE & COMPANY

85 York St.
Portland, ME 04101
quinceandco.com

SHIBUI KNITS LLC

1500 NW 18th, Ste. 110
Portland, OR 97209
shibuiknits.com

**TAHKI-STACY CHARLES
INC./FILATURA DI CROSA**

70-60 83rd St., Bldg. 112
Glendale, NY 11385
tahkistacycharles.com
In Canada: Diamond Yarn

**WESTMINSTER FIBERS/
ROWAN**

8 Shelter Dr.
Greer, SC 29650
and
10 Roybridge Gate, Ste. 200
Vaughan, Ontario
Canada L4H 3M8
westminsterfibers.com

bibliography, blogs, and websites

BOOKS

A., Cookie. *Knit. Sock. Love.* Mountain View, California: One Leg Press, 2010.

Atkinson, Jenny. *A Handknit Romance: 22 Vintage Designs with Lovely Details.* Loveland, Colorado: Interweave, 2012.

Bernard, Wendy. *Custom Knits 2: More Top-down and Improvisational Techniques.* New York: STC Craft, 2011.

Budd, Ann. *Sock Knitting Master Class: Innovative Techniques + Patterns from Top Designers.* Loveland, Colorado: Interweave, 2011.

Chanin, Natalie. *Alabama Studio Sewing + Design: A Guide to Hand-Sewing an Alabama Chanin Wardrobe.* New York: STC Craft, 2012.

Clark, Mel. *Knitting Everyday Finery: Practical Designs for Dressing Up in Little Ways.* North Pomfret, Vermont: Trafalgar Square Books, 2012.

Durham, Teva. *Loop-d-Loop Lace: More than 30 Novel Lace Designs for Knitters.* New York: Stewart, Tabori & Chang, 2011.

Eckman, Edie. *The Crochet Answer Book: Solutions to Every Problem You'll Ever Face; Answers to Every Question You'll Ever Ask.* North Adams, Massachusetts: Storey Publishing, 2005.

Griffin-Grimes, Kristeen. *French Girl Knits: Innovative Techniques, Romantic Details, and Feminine Designs.* Loveland, Colorado: Interweave, 2009.

Irwin, Laura. *Boutique Knits: 20+ Must-Have Accessories.* Loveland, Colorado: Interweave, 2008.

Japel, Stefanie. *Mom & Me Knits: 20 Pretty Projects for Mothers and Daughters.* San Francisco: Chronicle Books, 2012.

Leapman, Melissa. *Mastering Color Knitting: Simple Instructions for Stranded, Intarsia, and Double Knitting.* New York: Potter Craft, 2010.

Lewis, Susanna E. *Knitting Lace: A Workshop with Patterns and Projects.* Pittsville, Wisconsin: Schoolhouse Press, 2009.

MacDonald, Cecily Glowik, and Melissa LaBarre. *New England Knits: Timeless Knitwear with a Modern Twist.* Loveland, Colorado: Interweave, 2010

McGowan, Kristina. *Modern Top-down Knitting: Sweaters, Dresses, Skirts & Accessories Inspired by the Techniques of Barbara Walker.* New York: STC Craft, 2010.

Mucklestone, Mary Jane. *200 Fair Isle Motifs: A Knitter's Directory.* Loveland, Colorado: Interweave, 2011.

Orne, Michele Rose. *Inspired to Knit: Creating Exquisite Handknits.* Loveland, Colorado: Interweave, 2008.

Paden, Shirley. *Knitwear Design Workshop: A Comprehensive Guide to Handknits.* Loveland, Colorado: Interweave, 2010.

Radcliffe, Margaret. *The Knitting Answer Book: Solutions to Every Problem You'll Ever Face; Answers to Every Question You'll Ever Ask.* North Adams, Massachusetts: Storey Publishing, 2005.

Samsøe, Lene Holme. *Essentially Feminine Knits: 25 Must-Have Chic Designs.* Loveland, Colorado: Interweave, 2012.

ONLINE SOURCES

brooklyntweed.net

blog.yarn.com

chicknits.com

cocoknits.com

crochetbyfaye.blogspot.com

goknitinyourhat.blogspot.com

kimhargreaves.co.uk

knitgrrl.com

knitspot.com

knittinghelp.com

knittingdaily.com

margauxelena.typepad.com

masondixonknitting.com

planetpurl.com

ravelry.com

pinterest.com

techknitting.blogspot.com

blog.thecrochetdude.com

thehookandi.com

the-panopticon.blogspot.com

soulemama.com

theshetlandtrader.com

vickiehowell.com

westknits.com

wendyknits.net

yarnharlot.com

MY WEBSITES

bellefrancetours.com: Artisan Adventures in France

etsy.com/shop/FrenchGirlOrganics: Organic Apothecary and Cuisine Shoppe

frenchgirlcooks.wordpress.com: Recipes and Mediterranean Cuisine

frenchgirlknits.com: Knitting Patterns

pinterest.com/frenchorganics: Creative Online Inspiration Board

index

Not sure what to knit next? *We have a few ideas.*

French Girl Knits

Innovative Techniques, Rom
Details, and Feminine De

Kristeen Griffin-Grime

ISBN 978-1-59668-069-
$24.95

Boutique Knits

+ Must Have Accessories

Laura Irwin

ISBN 978-1-59668-073-9
$21.95

INTERWEAVE KNITS

From cover to cover, *Interw*
presents great projects for
advanced knitter. Every iss
captivating smart designs,
easy-to-understand illustr
lively articles sure to insp

daily

, an online community
n for knitting. You'll get a
patterns, projects store,
tes, galleries, tips and
Sign up for *Knitting Daily*